Acclaim for
FROM THE GROUND UP:
DIGITAL FUNDRAISING FOR NONPROFITS

"Brock has taken solid fundraising strategy and brought it to life through a real-world guide to digital fundraising. In plain language, Brock is providing tactical and practical advice, rooted in insights that will drive results. This is a must-read for fundraisers."
–MAEVE STRATHY

"...a welcome addition to nonprofit literature."
–JASON SHIM

"Brock provides an easy-to-digest essential overview of the digital tools that can complement age-old best practice in fundraising and help you raise more!"
–SARAH WILLEY, CFRE, MA, SMS

"Brock shares the wisdom he's acquired through years of research and gives you the practical knowledge he's gained by creating highly successful digital campaigns. You'll avoid beginners' mistakes and be launching your own winning campaigns in no time."
–DENNY YOUNG, MA

FROM THE GROUND UP:

DIGITAL FUNDRAISING FOR NONPROFITS

FUNDAMENTALS THAT WILL SERVE YOU
WELL FOR YEARS TO COME.

BROCK WARNER, CFRE (HE/HIM)

Tangram Editions

First Edition, September 2020

© 2020 by Brock Warner, CFRE

ISBN: 978-0-9809836-1-6

hello@brockwarner.ca
www.brockwarner.ca

Acknowledgements:

This book would not be possible without the support of my incredible wife Mary and my children Emmylou and Stella. To the many friends, family, peers, coworkers and mentors past and present, thank you all for your patience, compassion, belief and encouragement.

As my co-professor at Humber College, Tara Irwin, CFRE has helped tremendously to inform and improve on the best practices throughout this book with her many years of experience. Thank you Tara!

Special thanks to Holly H. Paulin for her keen eye and tireless efforts as my editor, and to Mikael Hansson, Jason Shim, Stephanie Highfield, Michelle Lee-Garbe, Kelsey Watson, Nicole Kallmeyer, Jay Onrait and Mimi Maxwell for your invaluable advice and input as this book took shape.

"The biology of purpose
keeps my nose above the surface."
— Brian Eno

INTRODUCTION

S ome things never change, right? Well, close. It only seems like it. In our digital age, there are more trends by the day, and each fad comes and goes so quickly that it feels like the world has moved on by the time you catch up. Chasing fads is exhausting, unproductive, and, perhaps most damaging of all, it's a distraction from the fundamentals that attract far less attention but wield far more power and influence.

We live and work in a world composed of layers. There are visible outer layers that get all the attention.

Those outer layers are the fashionable trends, flashy ideas, and headline news. Peel back those layers though, and the deeper we go, the slower the rate of change. As this rate of change declines, something else increases: importance. It's a concept Stewart Brand, Brian Eno and Danny Hillis have evangelized for decades through their work with the Long Now Foundation: what changes quickly gets all the attention, while what moves slowly has all the power.

Pause for a moment and think about the fast-moving layers in your life, the stuff that disappears as quickly as it arrives. Fashion. Latte flavours. Viral videos. Pop music. Apps. Fad diets. Flossing (the dance, not the other kind!). Besides a bit of fun and water cooler conversation, did any of these make a meaningful change in your life? If we were building a home, it's the latest coat of paint, or the pictures we've hung on the walls.

Now, consider the slow-moving layers in your life. The things that change at a painfully slow, possibly imperceptible pace. Your retirement savings. Public policy. Transit infrastructure. Wars. Medical research. These deeply entrenched systems that we interact with every day dictate our quality of life, the lives of our children, grandchildren and so on. These deep layers wield a shocking amount of power in our lives. In our house building analogy, the slowest moving layers would be the ground we build on and the initial foundation.

This way of looking at the world as being made up of slow-moving layers beneath fast-moving layers is easily applied to the ways in which you might effectively design, manage and oversee digital fundraising in your nonprofit—you need to build from the ground up. You need to get comfortable with those slow-moving layers that hold all of the power, but get none of the attention. I've written this book to share what more than a decade of front-line digital fundraising has taught me and what has lasted the test of time.

Each chapter of this book is meant to interlock with the previous chapter or section. We'll start with basic, fundamental concepts and definitions in *Section I: Understand It*. In *Section II: Design It*, we'll begin to put them to use as we design and plan the more tangible, visible pieces of your digital fundraising program. In *Section III: Build It*, we'll pick up speed by diving deeper into strategy, and developing a critical eye that will serve you well as you venture into *Section IV: Burn it Down*. There, we'll look at how, where, when and why you might want to set fire to your current under-performing program and build a new one from the ground up.

Throughout this book, you'll find simple, stripped-down definitions and explanations of terms and concepts you need to know. These are akin to an architect's drawings and blueprints, giving you the essential information to go from nothing to something on your journey toward building a dream home.

There were a several factors that pushed me to write this book. The biggest is that over several years as a professor at Humber College, in the country's leading postgraduate fundraising management course, I've been able to develop, adapt and revise all the content you'll find in this book based on how it is received by students at the time, and again based on feedback from graduates on what has—or has not—served them well on the job. I tend to start off the course by giving students a glimpse at some of the widely-held beliefs and practices that our nonprofit sector holds about digital fundraising:

> *"Digital? That's something marketing handles.*
> *"Email appeals are for small gifts."*
> *"Major donors don't want to get our emails."*
> *"Our social media followers don't give."*
> *"If we just keep doing great work, people will find us."*

Sound familiar? I've certainly heard them all at one point. But, by the time you finish this book I'm certain that you'll be confidently proclaiming:

> *"Online donors are some of our best prospects for major and planned giving."*
> *"If major donors don't want our regular emails, they'll either tell us directly or they'll unsubscribe."*
> *"How do we know our Facebook followers don't give? Let's investigate that and find out for certain."*
> *"If our website isn't converting visitors to donors, it's not doing its job."*

Today's reality for every nonprofit is that "digital" no longer stands alone as a tactic, team, department or strategy within a fundraising program. It runs deep through the walls of this house you're building, so deep you might forget it's even there—until it stops working. But, it's also the type of work that, if consistently maintained and upgraded, you'll be able to look back with pride and astonishment at what you've been able to accomplish.

Digital fundraising in its simplest form is *the use of online tools to enable, or enhance, philanthropy and volunteerism.* This is where we'll start, and if you stick with me to the end, you'll be forging ahead in your digital fundraising program in no time.

SECTION I:
UNDERSTAND IT

This is a black box: ■

Things go in, something happens, then something comes out. If we knew what was happening inside that box, it wouldn't be a black box. In the software engineering world, black boxes are the parts of an application or program that are confidential and proprietary. In aviation, a flight data recorder is often called an airplane's "black box" even though it isn't black, or a box. We call it a black box, because assuming there are no survivors, the black box contains the answers to solving a mystery.

For a lot of fundraisers, digital fundraising is a black box. I'm not saying they don't believe that it works, or that they aren't fully aware of the fact that donors are giving more frequently, and in higher amounts, online.

What these fundraisers don't understand is *how* this happens.

Not yet knowing how something works is perfectly fine. What is not fine is an unwillingness to look inside the box. But that's not you. Because you're holding this book, you've already opened the box.

Welcome.

This first step toward understanding something is to name it, so let's stick with the simple, broad definition of digital fundraising that we used just a few pages ago: *the use of online tools to enable, or enhance, philanthropy and volunteerism.* That's our first plumb line, and it's a perfect tool for the job because it's broad, it's not specific to any one platform or tool, and not bound to one specific outcome or goal. Heck, it's not even specific to raising money. It's the empty plot of land we need to start building on.

1.
WHERE WE STAND

I f we're going to build a sturdy foundation of digital fundraising knowledge, language and expertise then we need to have a strong understanding of the "land" we're about to build on. Background and context matter, and both are essential if we want to build something that lasts. Let's start unpacking who we're building for, where and how they use online technology, and why this knowledge can increase your digital fundraising program's efficiency, effectiveness, relevancy and impact.

A logical starting point and essential background is an understanding of truly how common internet access and social media usage is nowadays, because it confirms that your current donors are very likely active online, and that your future donors will absolutely be online. Pew Research's Spring 2019 Global Attitudes Survey (published in early 2020) gives us the most up-to-date evidence to support that Canada, the US and

UK have long passed the tipping point in favour of internet and social media usage. All but a small fraction of respondents between 18 and 49 report being at least occasional internet users. Social media participation is on the rise in all demographics—the 65+ age group ranges from 48% (UK) to 58% (Canada), and none of the 18–35 demographics dip below 79% participation.

It's not enough to just know that our current and future donors are highly active online though. We need to lean in a bit closer to see what they are doing while they're logged on, especially as it relates to charitable giving. Available data shows online giving has continued its trend of year-over-year growth that has been consistently ticking upward for a decade now. Blackbaud's 2019 Charitable Giving Study, which gathers donation data from over 5,200 US charities, reported a 6.8% increase in online giving over 2018, and on average, online giving made up 8.7% of total fundraising revenue for these organizations. Smaller charities (> $1M) had the highest proportion of their fundraising revenue from online sources, at 14.1%. The signals here are coming through loud and clear: online giving is not an insignificant piece of an organization's fundraising puzzle, and even more so if you're a smaller or newer organization.

What are people doing when they go online? How do they interact with one another and brands they support? What do they consume? What are their concerns (if any) around permission, privacy, truth in advertising, etc.? These behaviours and values—

amongst many other factors—directly inform what they see: the highly-personalized advertisements, curated search results, optimized product images, and more. The reality we find ourselves in now is that there is no longer a single shared experience on the web. There are millions of personalized, unique experiences happening inside every moment of every day. This is why digital fundraisers like you need to understand fundamental, objective best practice as opposed to subjective opinions and assumptions. If the final approval of your campaign hinges on the subjective opinions of one person, then you're only designing for an audience of one. The end result will be that you've alienated the majority of your supporter base, and raised less money for your cause as a result.

A baseline that you and your team should meet, which this book should equip you with, is to understand:

1. How traditional principles of philanthropy and fundraising can be enhanced with an integrated strategy that employs digital marketing and social media tools.

2. How to critically analyze both design and content across a variety of digital channels including websites, social media, email, blogs, video and digital advertising.

3. The ideal components of a prospect or donor's journey, specifically with respect to digital.

Establishing a baseline of digital fundraising knowledge throughout your fundraising team is one of the few ways to future-proof your charity. COVID-19 and the sweeping changes it has made to our daily lives aside, a second generation of digital natives (Generation Z, born in the late 1990s–early 2000s) is entering the workforce. Our donors' familiarity and fluency with digital and social media has to be considered at every stage of design and planning within of a comprehensive, integrated fundraising strategy.

Regardless of what generational bracket you or your donors might fall into, COVID-19 has undoubtedly altered how we all interact and communicate with family, friends, co-workers and companies. The pandemic has rapidly accelerated the need for digital-first strategies, in turn making digital fundraising best practice a skill set that should not be siloed within any single person, team or department. *Everyone* in your organization who has any level of responsibility whatsoever for raising funds should understand how to effectively engage with their donors or volunteers digitally. Even specialists in major gifts, legacy fundraising, special events, volunteer management or database management can benefit from an objective understanding—as opposed to a subjective "I don't like it, therefore it won't work" understanding—of what works and why, what doesn't work and why, and what is worth testing. From this shared understanding, we can create a plan that everyone on your team can interpret and act on.

Standardizing how you measure, manage and integrate digital strategies is thankless work, but it's absolutely necessary. Charities with an over-reliance on in-person events have struggled during the pandemic, as have entire sectors that have seen donations dry up. This is due in part to the massive economic contraction that resulted in millions of temporary and permanent job losses, but also to a deep shift in our routines and a heightened awareness (for some) about material excess and spending habits.

There are some seismic cultural shifts that are underway online, and they are adding new vital layers to our digital landscape. For example, Black Lives Matter burst into existence in 2013 in response to the acquittal of Trayvon Martin's killer. Since then, it has rapidly matured into an established, reputable, and formal charity in the US, UK and Canada. Black Lives Matter is in my opinion the best example we have of a movement that is effectively harnessing the energy, passion and enthusiasm that initially coalesced on social media. The first law of thermodynamics—that energy can neither be created nor destroyed, it can only be transferred or changed from one form to another—is in full effect here. Black Lives Matter didn't create the passion for justice and for the desire to end white supremacy. Black Lives Matter brought this energy together and directed it with intent and purpose.

What's far more common than capturing energy and coordinating efforts is seeing these surges of energy on social media fracture into many smaller, more dispersed initiatives. We saw this happen with the Occupy Wall Street movement, with people occupying public spaces all over the world to draw attention to the massive, and widening, global wealth inequality. The movement had a clear villain: the 1%. It had a simple, disruptive tactic: occupy public spaces. For a few exciting months, it seemed like we were on the cusp of a spectacular societal change. But when local governments dismantled the tents, cleared out occupiers, and re-sodded the grass, the energy of the movement was fragmented and dispersed in thousands of different directions. But we're still hearing echoes of it, nearly a decade later. In labour movements fighting with renewed vigour and a more youthful membership, in progressive political ideologies led by women of colour, and in the intersectional third wave of feminism that is creating space for voices and experiences that for centuries have been marginalized and silenced.

All of this is what lies behind, below, and ahead of us. It is complex and demanding. But, with the willingness to roll up our sleeves and enough knowledge to get moving, the opportunities are endless.

2.
THINKING IN SYSTEMS

The number of ways we can solicit donations only grows. It never, ever shrinks. Email didn't replace direct mail.

Brochures didn't disappear when websites arrived. Text messaging did not destroy telefundraising. As tactics, tools and platforms pile up on top of one another, we tech-savvy digital fundraisers have to hone and maintain our ability to wade through these weeds of ever-increasing uncertainty and complexity. We need to be able to embrace it. Plan for it. Leverage it. Tolerance for ambiguity is a sign of maturity in our lives, which includes our fundraising careers, because the digital ecosystem we operate within is constantly evolving. It has a food chain, complete with predators and prey. It has seasonal shifts. It gives and supports life, but it also generates and disposes of waste.

In a food chain, each organism fits into a "trophic level" based on what it eats, and what eats it. The sun at the bottom, because it feeds the plants, and apex predators at the top. This however is a vast oversimplification because in fact there are food chains—or systems—repeatedly nested deep within each other. One such nested ecosystem is the type created by what ecologists refer to as "ecosystem engineers." The beaver is the poster child of ecosystem engineers. The act of harvesting sticks and mud to build their dams alters their surroundings so drastically that they create new, smaller ecosystems in which other organisms thrive.

Fundraisers—especially digital fundraisers—are ecosystem engineers. We use what limited resources we have to fashion a space that thrives on a healthy give-and-take relationship. We provide a sense of purpose, active participation in solving a problem, and we lighten karmic burdens. In return, we're the recipients of money, expertise, volunteer hours, etc.

Your charity—your ecosystem—very likely spun out of a much larger ecosystem. That's not to say it can't be the catalyst for systems-level change though. StopGap is a Canadian charity that builds sturdy, portable, brightly-coloured ramps for businesses with a single-step entry. This small intervention dramatically and immediately improves accessibility for people who use wheelchairs, walkers, canes, strollers, etc. It's an elegant solution to a specific problem, and StopGap is engineering their ecosystem within a larger system of accessibility regulation and enforcement (or lack of it) in our cities and towns. Throughout Canada, these ramps spark debate and conversation about whether or not they contravene by-laws and if they meet safety standards. These debates shed light on issues like the sorely-lacking enforcement of building standards for accessibility, and the cost-prohibitive nature of retrofitting an existing small business to code. Debates like these, harnessing energy and focusing it in a strategic way, are our best chances at rapid, transformational societal systems change.

Systems Thinking is a discipline in its own right, but throughout this book we'll use it broadly, and define it as *an understanding of a system by examining the linkages and interactions between the components that comprise the entirety of that defined system.* It's a mental model that can help you navigate complex challenges and situations, and a tool in your chest. Like a Swiss Army knife, it should be kept close, and used often.

If you remember nothing else from that definition, remember this: **linkages and interactions**. You don't need to understand the complete inner workings of every component in a system in order to be a systems thinker. What you do need to know is just enough about each component to understand the effects each might induce on another component.

For example, I didn't go to medical school, so I don't understand how my brain triggers a hunger pang, and what is causing me to get so irritable as a result. But I understand what the signal means, and that if I ignore it I'll only get more hangry as a result. I don't understand how every component of a combustion engine works, but I know what happens when my gas tank is empty, or if I don't change the oil on time. I know what happens when I have a flat tire, worn brakes, or a dead battery. And if all else fails, I know how to call a tow truck.

As new tools, platforms, and channels roll out by the day, you'll more often need to pause and consider what new interactions and effects they'll have on your activities and strategies. You don't have to master every new tool right away, but an understanding of what it does, who it's for, and how it works goes a long way in helping you understand how it might fit alongside what is already working for you. Going all-in on the latest social media platform won't be a wise use of time, effort or money for the majority of charities. But for some, it may be just the opportunity you've been looking for to reach a new audience, or to showcase your charity's programming where you know it will resonate. Yes, this means you might have to sign up for a personal account and play around. Yes, you might have to actually talk to some young people to ask what they like about it, how they use it, and why. Yes, you might have to read some blogs about it. After all that, you won't be an expert, but you'll know enough to make an informed decision about why it is or isn't worth your time—rather than broad, generalized assumptions.

Simply understanding the dynamic, ambiguous nature of systems is an accomplishment. Fundraisers have a tendency to sort new technology in one of two ways: a game-changer that everyone should be using, or a distraction akin to a child's toy that "real" fundraisers need not pay attention to. Beware of these strict binary distinctions, and don't be surprised if the source of these opinions is trying to sell you a product or service. Life—and fundraising—is rarely so simple.

3.
CHANNELS

There are some basic definitions we need to cover. These are the deep, slow-moving layers we discussed in the introduction that get none of the attention but have all of the power. Stick with me, and this knowledge will serve you well for the rest of your career.

A channel is *how your message is transmitted to your target audience*. It's the string, pulled taut between two tin cans. The string is the channel, because it transmits the message. For our purposes, the channel does not create the message—it simply carries it.

The most common digital fundraising channels your donors will be using are:

1. **Email**: This "push" channel is effective because of the control you have to determine the timing and

content, as well the options to customize, personalize, and segment.

2. **Social**: This channel is most effective for community building, discussion, and organizing. As a fundraising tool, it will most often raise the majority of donations by directing people to your website or donation form, via a great post, advertisement or video. The US has far more opportunities for users to donate directly to a charity within an app, such as Facebook Fundraisers, Instagram donate buttons, and until recently Snapcash in Snapchat. At the time of writing this, in Canada there is no donation functionality within Instagram, and while Facebook Fundraisers is available, it is powered by a clunky integration with the PayPal Giving Fund that limits administrative controls for the charity.

3. **Text Message (or SMS)**: This channel is most effective when the people you are texting have specifically requested this form of communication. For example, if the Red Cross has a list of people that want to know via text message when they can help a disaster effort, text message recipients would likely see this as a major benefit to their monthly commitment, rather than an annoyance. **Text-to-Give** is the most common fundraising tactic via SMS, where you promote the ability for anyone to *"Text ABCDE to 12345 now to give $5"*. In this scenario, the gift is billed directly to the donor's

phone bill. This works best when you have <u>massive</u> reach, e.g. U2 is going to promote it on stage at each stop of their tour. An emerging strategy is the **value exchange** wherein you promote a non-donation offer, such as, *"Text STROKE to 12345 for your free guide to recognizing the signs of a stroke."* In this scenario, the sender receives a follow-up text with a download link, and the charity will likely follow up with an ask.

4. **Website**: This channel is effective because, if designed properly, it makes a compelling case for charitable support, demonstrates accountability and trustworthiness, and promotes ways for visitors to help. It should also make it easy for new visitors to subscribe to your email list, which will give you the ability to continue communicating with them.

5. **Search**: Every search engine, fundamentally, allows people to search for content related to, or specifically for your charity. There are a wide variety of factors that increase or decrease the likelihood of your website appearing at the top of a search engine's results. The entirety of these factors is a black box, but what never changes is the fact that a website that is clearly written and kept up-to-date is will always be a sound strategy to build upon.

If you've been around marketing and fundraising a few years, you could probably add to this list. Different sectors also speak about channels differently. Were we selling garage doors or frying pans, you might define channels as retailers, distributors, and wholesalers. But, we're not. We are trying to raise money online, and these are the fundamental channels you need to know.

In terms of online fundraising from individuals, you'll raise most of your money through email and your website. No other digital fundraising channel comes close to directly raising as much money for charities as an email program that welcomes in new subscribers, shares great stories on a consistent schedule, and asks for support in a clear, compelling manner. This 'push' channel is effective because it offers charities the ability to control the timing, content, audience segmentation, and in many cases, personalization.

If a charity is investing a tonne of time and effort in their digital program, but are raising very little money online, it is likely that, rather than starting with a robust email strategy, they have opted to focus primarily on social media instead. The popularity and potential reach of social media makes this incredibly tempting, but social media for brands is very much a pay-to-play marketplace. A Facebook account may be free but I can assure you that if you want to reach 100% of your own followers you'll need to pay for advertising to do so. On Facebook, an update that you simply post to your page without paying to increase visibility—or, "reach"—will only be displayed to a small percentage of your followers, likely less than 10% of people who have liked your page. This is what we call "organic reach." Facebook has an ever-evolving proprietary algorithm—a black box—that favours different posts depending on the content, timing, and engagement. The latter, engagement, is one of the most dependable ways to expand the reach of a post. The more authentic interactions, such as likes, shares and comments there are from your community, the more likely Facebook's algorithm will suggest it to others.

While social media restricts or controls access to your community of supporters, email marketing does not. Email allows you to proactively create and send messages to your entire list of subscribers. Not every recipient will open the email, but you will know exactly how many, and in Section II we'll dive deep into how you can continually measure and optimize your email program to move those open rates up.

If you want your emails to raise money, you have to have a website that pulls its weight. You'll most likely be sending visitors to a donation form, a landing page, or some other form of content on your website. The work you put into your website—and we'll be covering this in detail in Section II—will provide a fantastic ROI for your email program.

The time and effort you'll invest in your website will fall into two basic buckets: helping your website to be easily found by someone who has an interest in your mission, and, once it is found, ensuring it does what the visitor expects it to. In Section II, we'll dig deeper into both of these in our *Hard Working Websites* chapter.

I do have an important caveat to all of the above. There are always exceptions and outliers that defy my experience and advice. There are charities that have raised fistfuls of cash with Facebook Fundraisers, crowdfunding, text-to-give, and celebrity endorsements. All the more reason to measure and track the metrics that are most important to you. Trying to replicate the success of an outlier is a bit like buying lottery tickets as a retirement plan. My advice to you is to get started with the tough, long-term work of investing in your own skills, and in your organization's ability to execute the fundamentals flawlessly.

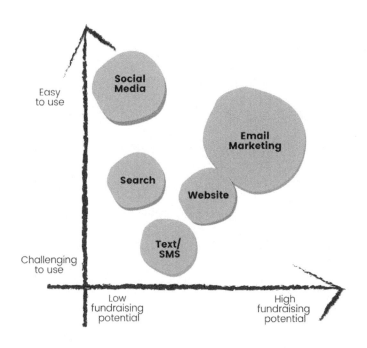

4.
OFFERS

A nchoring every message that you send—whether you've realized it or not—is an offer of some kind. Sometimes it's obvious, sometimes not.

To put a finer point on it, offers are *the product, ask, or message used to anchor your communication.* An offer should always strive to be valuable to your audience, because it is among the few counterweights we can add to the balance of power in our favour. If donors, supporters and sponsors feel like they are carrying the weight of a one-sided relationship, they won't stick around for long.

The latter form of offers mentioned above—the less obvious, more nebulous sort—are like bass notes in your symphony. They provide weight, atmosphere, and are essential to a well-rounded harmony. Your brand voice, and the cadence of your posts (weekly, daily, or more often) are an offer, in so far as they either fulfill or conflict with what a supporter was expecting. Some supporters want to be inspired. Some want to learn. Some want to be kept abreast of international events, and others want to assuage guilt.

The more obvious, material examples of offers are what your digital channels will often have on full display. The most common examples include (but are not limited to):

Petitions: These, which we dive deeper into in Section III, show that your charity is approaching your particular issue or service gap with a multi-pronged approach that goes beyond direct service delivery. Petitions are also great lead magnets, provided you are collecting the necessary permissions when the person adds their name to your petition.

Blog posts: Website design and content strategy have been steadily moving away from including a blog or news section as the adoption of social media has increased. Nonetheless, many charities still maintain a blog or news section. Each time you update, be sure to maximize the reach of these articles by cross-posting updates on your social media channels, and possibly with a dedicated email blast.

Shareable video or photos: On social media, shareability is a key factor in maximizing engagement. It's what will unlock access to new audiences when your core audience circulates it to their friends, family and coworkers. Shareable video needs to evoke an emotion, whether it's joy, shock, disbelief or pride. Overlaying text on a video is increasingly popular, not only because it makes the content more accessible, but also because many platforms by default will autoplay a video on mute. When your goal is shareability, photos with a simple key statistic, quote or statement tend to gain the most traction.

Contests: If used in moderation, and in a way that feels true to your brand, a contest can be a great way to boost engagement on social media. A corporate sponsor may appreciate the additional brand recognition for what might be a relatively small in-kind donation of product, and if the contest is tied into a fundraising activity like a peer-to-peer event, these contests can have a powerful multiplier effect. Be sure to brush up on your provincial or state lottery and gaming laws to ensure you're in compliance.

White papers: Some charities take for granted the amount of access they have to experiences and data that are of great interest to the people who support their work. If you find yourself with a larger-than-normal amount of data on your hands, consider packaging it up into a 2- to 3-page white paper that can be downloaded and circulated. The benefit of a white paper is that, by definition, it isn't a peer-reviewed journal submission. It is, per Wikipedia, "an authoritative report or guide that informs readers concisely about a complex issue and presents the issuing body's philosophy on the matter." There are many free or inexpensive tools and website widgets that allow you to require an email address to download the paper, if email collection is one of your primary reasons for offering the research.

Invitations, events and exclusive access: A large proportion of people who support charities want active, in-person opportunities to engage with the work you do. Event invitations can be spiced up with video, maybe with a celebrity ambassador or a charity founder delivering the message. You can also incentivize your audience to take action with perks like pre-sale access to special events, discounts in your store, or virtual town halls with a founder or celebrity supporter.

Being thoughtful and intentional about what you are offering current and future donors in every message you send is essential to growing your digital fundraising program. These offers reinforce your charity's purpose, and communicate to donors how, when and why their support is vital to achieving your mission.

5.
TOOLS, PLATFORMS AND INTEGRATIONS

I n a digital fundraising context, **tools**—and increasingly, entire platforms—enable you to prepare and send your message to an audience. If the string between two tin cans is your channel, then the tin cans you're speaking into are the tools.

The differences between a tool and platform can be admittedly blurry. Typically, a tool is a uni-tasker, meaning it does one thing, and (hopefully) does it very well. A **platform** ties together many tools into one place and gives you the ability to execute tasks across those various platforms from one control centre.

We would all benefit from having only one system in our organization that houses and deploys all our fundraising, marketing, communications, accounting, and data/gift processing. But, the reality is that an organization will often have several platforms knitted together.

In your charity, you'll need to manage one or more of the following, including:

1. **Donor data** – biographical, contact information, preferences, deceased or living, relationships, school, workplace and job title.

2. **Donation data** – gift dates, gift amounts, appeals sent, receipts issued, payment methods.

3. **Events** – registrations, ticket sales, RSVPs, ticketing pages, calendars of events, sponsors, invitations.

4. **Research** – past, current and potential funder contact information, grant opportunities, wealth ratings, company filings, news clippings, call reports)

5. **Your Website** – a content management system, blog and news entries, job postings, volunteer opportunity listings.

6. **Social Media** – social media scheduler, listening services, analytics reporting and tracking.

7. **Email Marketing** – eNewsletters, automated emails, promotions, fundraising appeals.

8. **Content Marketing** – podcasts, blogs, white papers, petitions, videos.

9. **Advertising** – search, display, video and social media.

10. **Surveys** – design, conditional questions, response collection, feedback, analysis.

Each of the above organizational needs has its own marketplace of competitors vying for you to test, subscribe to, or purchase their tool. In my experience, there is not a single product or service that can serve all those needs for you—despite a salesperson's best efforts to convince you otherwise.

Because no single platform will meet every one of your needs perfectly ad infinitum, it is critical that you evaluate whether or not your patchwork of platforms can easily pass information between one another. This is called **integration**: *the ability to pass information between separate platforms.*

Integrations can save you time, which in turn saves you money. Examples of common integrations:

⇢ Email signup forms on your website + your email marketing tool.

⇢ Online donation forms + your donor database

⇢ Your website + Google Analytics

⇢ Accounting software + your data visualization software

Here's one example of tools, platforms and integration in a simple digital lead generation campaign:

To promote World Oceans Day, we'll publish a research paper and share it on Facebook. To download it, you'll have to provide an email address and it will be emailed to you right away.

The offer = a research paper

The channel = social media

The platform(s) = Facebook Business Manager (or possibly just as a page administrator), as well as an email marketing platform (e.g. MailChimp)

The integration(s) = Facebook is passing the collected email addresses to the email marketing platform

The effort and investment in finding and setting up platforms that integrate with one another will pay for itself many times over. Depending on what components you've assembled, you may have simple, built-in integrations that you can use, you may have to build them yourself (if you have that level of technical ability), or you may have to outsource the work. But once in place, integrations will save you time, and you'll have all sorts of new opportunities and paths to explore with the linkages and interactions that you've uncovered—not to mention the extra time you'll have now that you're no longer exporting, formatting, and importing spreadsheets.

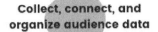Collect, connect, and organize audience data

Increase and improve your personalization, segmentation, and customization

Invite more meaningful engagement, and loyalty

Measure, track results, and test

Raise more money for your charity

6.
PROCESSING

So, your donor is ready to give. They head to your website, hit that donation button, enter all their personal and payment information, then they hit that last button to complete the transaction. It's at this brief moment—and it is quite literally just a moment for the donor—that an essential part of your digital fundraising ecosystem whirs to life: **donation processing**.

To securely transact funds, charities will use a third-party platform for their donation processing. These platforms can range from very basic, e.g., Stripe, Paypal, all the way up to highly-complex systems for large enterprises. Some of the more advanced features that come with additional costs might include the capability to issue custom e-receipts, a customizable design so that it blends seamlessly into your website, event ticketing, crowdfunding, and more. These larger solutions will often charge an annual licensing fee, as well as a small percentage (typically 1.5-3%) of each donation. Basic services may not charge monthly or annual fees, but will instead charge a higher percentage of each donation (4-10%). Larger solutions will often charge an annual licensing fee, and a smaller percentage.

In addition to the fees you will pay to your platform provider, you can expect to pay an unavoidable credit card fee as well. You may not see these charges when using the more basic processing platforms, where they often account for the Visa, MasterCard and American Express fees within the percentage they charge you. The larger processing platforms, because their clients are processing very large amounts of money, will typically include the credit card fees within a service agreement as separate line items.

There are a few more terms from the payment processing world that you should familiarize yourself with:

Every credit card transaction requires four active parties: the **merchant,** (your charity), the **customer**, (your donor or ticket buyer, etc.), the **issuing bank** that issued the customer's credit or debit card, and the **acquiring bank** (yours) that collects the funds from the issuing bank.

Payment Gateway: This the first stop in the payment processing system. It completes the initial checks to determine whether a credit card is valid. If the card is marked as invalid, the payment gateway will stop the transaction and notify the nonprofit.

Payment Processor: A payment processor is the company or provider that facilitates the sending and receiving of donations. A payment processor can offer a payment gateway, merchant account, ACH/direct debit options and credit card payments.

Issuing Bank (Issuer): The issuing bank is the financial institution that issues credit cards to consumers on behalf of the card networks (Visa, MasterCard, Amex, Discover). The issuer acts as the intermediary between the cardholder and the card network.

PCI Compliance: The Payment Card Industry (PCI) has set up data security standards (DSS) that any company that processes donations or transactions must follow. These standards keep consumer and donor data safe. Failure to comply can result in fines, penalties, and loss of payment processing capabilities. Payment processors will usually charge nonprofits a yearly PCI compliance fee to ensure their systems meet or exceed the standards.

Understanding these underlying mechanics is going to serve you well for a few reasons. One, there will be cost savings opportunities here as your program grows. If your charity is processing a large amount of money through your online platforms, then the costs of doing business can add up quickly. This knowledge will also help you troubleshoot issues as they arise, minimizing any system downtime which directly results in a loss of donations.

SECTION II:
DESIGN IT

L et's start as simply as possible with a shared definition of design, to set the stage for what's to come: *design is how you assemble components for a specific purpose*. Within this definition, "components" can refer to everything we covered in Section I, and more. You've got a lot of decisions to make in this crucial design stage when you start piecing together the 'how', 'when' and 'why' of your digital initiatives.

What we are not going to dive into is graphic design or web design beyond some basic usability and best practices. Doing these well is essential to and inextricable from your success, but there is a wealth of research and writing about this topic, so if this chapter resonates with you, go forth and dig into all the great work that others have published.

We started Section I with the mental model of systems thinking, to prepare you for managing complexity and change. In Section II, we'll cover the core principles of design thinking, a flexible methodology that puts your current and future donors at the centre of your design and decision-making process.

1.
DESIGN THINKING

So much of our fundraising revenue comes from traditional tactics, informed by "best practice." But, best practice *for whom*? Best practice *when*? Best practice *under what conditions*? Best practices *from where*?

Because of the variability that arises from each of those questions, "best practice" is overused and rarely accurate. Your next big idea—the game changer that sets you and your charity apart from your peers—is not likely to come by replicating what your peers are doing. Your next big idea is far more likely to come from doing the hard but incredibly important work of listening to your donors and other stakeholders, testing, measuring, and then starting the process all over again.

Does this sound familiar?

Step 1: Learn a best practice (a conference, a book)
Step 2: Replicate and adapt to your brand & budget
Step 3: Execute
Step 4: Measure against benchmarks
Step 5: Scrap it, repeat it, or maybe tweak something minor

There's nothing terribly wrong with that process—in fact there are plenty of situations where it is the right way to get from start to finish. However, it would be a mistake to think it's the only way to do so. This is where design thinking provides an alternative:

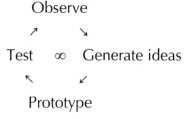

Explaining what design thinking is and how it can help you raise more money has at times, for me, felt like the most difficult part of design thinking. The linear process of project management is deeply ingrained in our training and daily practice. Here is how I typically break down the term to its component parts, and tie it back to the all-important donor experience that we are all striving to improve:

Design: *creating and refining a product or service*
   +

Thinking: *generating insights through observation*

=

Improved human (donor) experience

When we are using a design thinking methodology, we are generating insights to create something that improves human experience. There are some incredible benefits to giving this a try: to reduce risk and costs associated with launching new ideas, to learn faster, to capture and explore the mindsets and needs of your donors, to identify new needs-based opportunities, and to generate solutions that have major innovative potential, not just incremental tweaks.

OBSERVATION

If you're starting a project from scratch, you'll want to kick things off in what we describe as the observation phase. Here is where you need to define your challenge (easier said than done). Ideally, you've kicked off this process because a challenge or barrier has been brought forward by a donor or volunteer. Avoid the temptation to start with a typically quantifiable goal right off the bat, like "how might we improve our conversion rate 12% this quarter". At this stage, we want to explore the *why and how* of a problem, as well as the *what*.

Why and How = build loyalty, tell better stories, better engage young people

What = x increase in donors, response rates, ROI

We all need more donors, and higher response rates. But if we don't pair those desired outcomes with an activity like telling better stories, we lack the clarity we need to move onto the next stage—idea generation. Heading into the idea generation phase without a why and how leaves far too wide a playing field and won't produce the exciting and potentially effective solutions you're hoping for.

With a defined challenge, you'll next need to determine the audience that you'll be trying to engage, as well as how you might assemble a sample of these people when the time is right. For example, if you are designing an awareness campaign that is intended to reach pre-teens in your city, now is the time to start planning how to responsibly gather a fairly representative sample of actual pre-teens in a video call, focus group or in a survey.

Now, it's time to bring them together. And yes, this is before the idea generation phase. What we are doing at this stage is asking a few questions, but largely listening and probing where reasonable and respectful to do so. The pretext for this conversation could look something like this:

"Hi _____! We're prepping for our next campaign, and we thought we'd start by chatting with people like you to help get the ideas flowing, and to be sure what we produce is the type of campaign that you and people like you will be interested in."

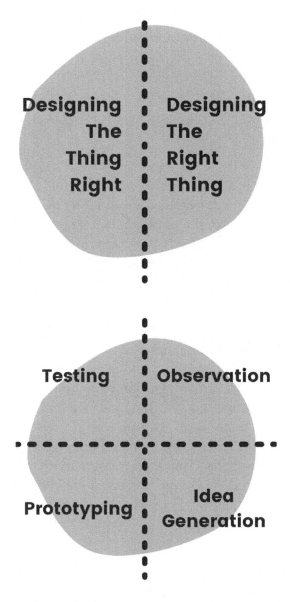

53

While you're having that friendly chat, we want to have our ears tuned for some specific data:

Values: What is important to them?
Aspirations: What do they want their life to look like?
Behaviours: What are their routines and habits?
Attributes: What do they look for in a charity, product, campaign, etc.?

Answers to these questions are incredibly rich with qualitative data. Whether by recording the interview then transcribing, or doing a brain dump of notes soon afterward, it's important that you capture all that you can. As you've collected an increasing number of interviews, you may start to see patterns emerge—capture that! These are some of your first glimpses of the direction in which your ideas and projects might go.

Here's a pitfall that you want to avoid: *confusing observations with insights*. You've heard me use both by now, but they are in fact quite different. Observations are your raw data, recorded objectively with as little analysis as possible (yet). Insights are interpretations of the data that lead to opportunities, and they emerge as connections begin to reveal themselves in the form of patterns. A great insight is actionable, whereas an observation is just that: an observation. Let's look at an example:

⋯➤ An **observation** would be that the response rate to the email appeal that detailed the advanced technology being used in our hospital was far lower than our average return. The objective data here is the response rate, and without more information it is unclear what next steps should be taken to bring the response rate up to normal levels.

⋯➤ An **insight** would be that technology for the sake of technology is not a motivator for giving. This insight is much more clearly actionable because we can see a challenge—how might we help donors see the benefits of medical technology in ways that motivates them to give?—and we have a sense of what needs to be done next.

IDEA GENERATION

Intentionally, the observation stage of the design thinking methodology is time consuming, challenging, and uncomfortable. But if you do it well, the rest of the process begins to fall in place because you've set yourself up for success. It's in this next phase—idea generation—when we start to explore possibilities for addressing your challenge with confidence and creativity.

Have you ever been invited to a brainstorming session, and within the first five minutes you're asked to spew out an endless amount of brilliant, funny, innovative ideas that are also on-brand, cost-effective, and not too risky? All of the above is painfully familiar. One way to minimize this is to make sure your brainstorm sessions have plenty of time set aside specifically for reviewing who your audience is, what you observed during your interviews and research, and what insights you've synthesized from the process so far. It's entirely possible that you'll need just as much time for this as you'll need for the brainstorming itself.

Here are five tips for hosting a great brainstorming session:

1. **Build a great sandbox** for participants to play in, by giving a clear and informed briefing.
2. **Avoid groupthink** when a good idea strikes by capturing, then pivoting conversation.
3. **Come prepared** with some tough "what if…?" and "but what about…?" questions.
4. **Bring more sticky notes** than you think you'll need, then put them to use.
5. **Bring in fresh eyes and ears** which might be volunteers, board members, even donors!

With a wall or whiteboard of ideas, some fully formed and some just breadcrumbs on the way to something great, you have a whole new task as the brainstorm host. If your team is fully or partially virtual, Miro is a simple and free virtual whiteboard tool worth testing. With your myriad of ideas, you'll want to begin sorting through ideas, either as a group or afterwards as the project lead, by asking the following:

- ☐ Does it make sense for our brand?
- ☐ Is it viable within our budget?
- ☐ Is this something our donors would want?
- ☐ Is this logistically and technically possible?
- ☐ Does it address our original challenge?

By passing your top ideas through these filters, some clear front runners will begin to emerge. As a group, select up to three of them to move into the prototype stage where they will begin to take shape.

PROTOTYPING

A prototype is an early, rough representation of an idea that is concrete enough for people to interact with, which will provide you incredibly rich data. If at all possible, it should be something that you can literally put into people's hands in order to observe their reactions, which will in turn help you to evaluate, refine and move towards the best solution. Prototypes should be as low-tech and low-cost as you can possibly manage, while still eliciting the reactions and interactions that you're hoping for from your demonstration. Think Sharpies, cardboard, Scotch tape, etc. Really.

There's no such thing as a perfect prototype—that might actually be an oxymoron. It's what you do with it, and what you learn from it that matters—despite its appearance. A great prototype should be something that allows you to quickly try lots of things, strip away what's not working, and refine what is. Remember, do not get attached to your prototype!

Examples of prototypes that a fundraiser might create are:

- A simple mockup of a website/landing page in PowerPoint.
- Outer envelope and insert mockups.
- Video storyboards.
- Roleplaying the experience of someone calling into your office and hearing the auto-attendant messages.
- Playing with new meeting formats.

During my time at War Child Canada, we wanted to develop a flexible, DIY fundraising concept and tool that would engage and appeal to younger donors. The first concepts for internal buy-in were made in MS Paint. With a green light from leadership, we hosted a focus group of students to talk about their charitable giving habits, amongst other things, and we showed them a mockup of a website we had whipped up in PowerPoint. On that homepage mockup we had a big (fake) button that said "Get Started Now" and we asked the students what they expect would happen after they clicked that button. Intentionally, we hadn't planned past that stage of the user experience, because we wanted to hear from our target audience what they expected, needed, and wanted to happen next. The answers helped us design and build 80% of the website's functionality and content. The first iteration of make.warchild.ca was far from perfect, but it was a living tool. Once live, we were able to repeat the process of showing it to young people and watching them interact with it in real time. Within eight months we did a significant redesign that vastly simplified the process, providing far fewer options, but a better user experience for what remained.

TESTING

With your new design thinking mindset, "testing" is what you used to call "finishing." This is when you finally get to release the tool, product or service to the world, beyond the small groups that helped generate ideas and interact with the many iterations of your prototype.

You are on a learning journey, not racing toward a finish line. You've breathed life into the project, and now you need to take good care of it. You'll want to do this by having specific quantitative measures like response rates, website analytics, etc. that you'll chart out in some form and review on a schedule. If possible, in equal measure, you should seek out some qualitative observations to validate assumptions and uncover new insights.

Chances are, one of those measures—analyzing quantitative data, versus gathering qualitative insights—will seem more intimidating than the other. That's normal. Acknowledge it, make a plan, and move forward. I think you'll be surprised by what you find.

The testing stage is where you'll truly find out if you've built something great on top of a strong foundation, if what you've built is in need of a few repairs, or if it's time to start from scratch. When you've really hit on something great, the data, feedback and results are going to tell you. Have fun with it!

※ ※ ※

This section would not be possible without the hard work and brilliant insights of Nicole Kallmeyer. Nicole and I co-presented a Design Thinking 101 session at a recent Association of Fundraising Professionals International Conference (ICON) in San Antonio, Texas. Thanks also to Jennie Winhall and Elaine Broe, instructors of Leading by Design at the Banff Centre for Arts and Creativity who first introduced me to these core design thinking concepts.

Above: 1 Using Microsoft Paint, the War Child Canada team mocked up some basic prototypes of how the "Make _____, Not War" brand may come to life.

Above: 2 Using Microsoft Powerpoint, a simple homepage was mocked up to share with a focus group of students.

Above: 3 The next iteration of the platform simplified the user experience, and provided more interactive tools.

IF WE ALLOW OUR SELF-CONGRATULATORY ADORATION OF TECHNOLOGY TO DISTRACT US FROM OUR OWN CONTACT WITH EACH OTHER, THEN SOMEHOW THE ORIGINAL AGENDA HAS BEEN LOST.

Jaron Lanier
Virtual Reality pioneer, Author, Artist

2.
HARD WORKING WEBSITES

━━━━━━━━━━━━━━━━━━━━━

I f you want to make the most of the hard work you've put into each component in Section I, don't overlook the role that a website has to play.

What I am not going to attempt to do in this book is to explain how to build a website, because it is highly unlikely that an organization's fundraiser will be tasked with creating a website from scratch. It is far more likely that you'll be asked for input, or to project manage a website redevelopment. When this inevitably happens, you'll want to wear your digital fundraiser hat, ensuring that none of these fundamentals are missed.

There are a handful of questions that donors of any size or type will expect your website to answer. Whether they're an existing major donor, a potential monthly donor, or a government agency researching prospective partners, the answers to the questions listed below are critical to their giving consideration process.

Ensure that your website **clearly** addresses each of the following questions (in no particular order):

- ☐ Is this a registered charity, and if so, what is the registration number?
- ☐ How do I contact the organization by email, phone or mail?
- ☐ What does this charity do, why, where and for whom?
- ☐ How do I give a donation?
- ☐ How do I subscribe to email updates?
- ☐ Is this charity fiscally responsible? Can I review their annual reports or audited financials?
- ☐ Who sits on their Board of Directors *right now*?
- ☐ Who is in charge?
- ☐ How are donations used?
- ☐ What does the organization need *right now*?
- ☐ What volunteer opportunities might exist, and how do I sign up for them?

Every one of the above is vital. Not one can be skipped. Below are some more website components that are fantastic, but less vital. Some may not be applicable or of value to your charity, or to your supporters.

- ☐ Blogs or news stories (and if you're going to use this feature, be sure you keep it relevant and updated).
- ☐ Profiles of donors, volunteers, supporters.
- ☐ Links to your social media accounts (but only if they are active!).
- ☐ Job postings.
- ☐ A shop for selling merchandise.
- ☐ Non-cash actions to take, e.g., sign a petition, mail a letter, etc.
- ☐ Awards, memberships and certifications.
- ☐ Other ways to give, e.g., in-kind, legacy, securities, etc.

Visitors find your website in a wide variety of ways—by searching relevant terms in a search engine like Google, by seeing a shared post or update on social media, word of mouth, TV ads, etc. While bringing new visitors to your website is vitally important, it is somewhat outside the domain of a fundraiser, and more so the responsibility of a marketer or search engine optimization (SEO) specialist.

Broadly, you can divide visitors into two buckets: those who have come with the intention to donate, and everyone else. For the first group, so long as you have a donation form that is easy to find and functions as intended, you don't need to lose sleep over the ways in which you can incrementally optimize their experience. The latter group is much more slippery and mysterious but offers a tremendous opportunity to attract new or reactivated donors.

I recommend spending more of your time and effort on the visitors that have arrived at your website simply to learn, rather than having come with a specific task in mind (e.g., to donate or volunteer). The most common ways to do this (in order of importance are):

1. **Capturing their email addresses** and permission to contact them.
2. **Capturing their name**, even just a first name, so that you can personalize those communications. Capturing more information will help, but don't ask for anything you don't plan to use.
3. **Using a tracking cookie** with permission so that you can target them with relevant advertisements at a later date. This practice is called "remarketing" or "retargeting" and when done well can be very effective at bringing visitors back who didn't give a donation, or provide their email.

Capturing email addresses is where every digital fundraiser needs to get creative. We have all seen variations on the simple "Subscribe for Updates!" form that collects dust in the footer of a website. A static form in a footer—or even better, a header—is not a mistake. What would be a mistake is relying entirely on that form to drive your list growth.

Here are just a few ideas for additional, creative ways to collect email addresses:

→ A quick, simple survey or quiz. If it's fun and playful, an ask for an email address and permission to keep in touch won't feel out of place.

→ A downloadable guide that relates to your cause and will be useful to the user. This might be a guide to recognizing the signs of a stroke that can be posted in a workplace, or a letter template for writing to a local politician.

→ A promise of pre-sale access to your special events, or special offers and discounts from your corporate partners.

MOBILE-FRIENDLY WEBSITES

Whether or not your website is mobile friendly—meaning it was either built specifically for mobile browsers, or it can detect that the visitor is on mobile and the content and layout changes accordingly—has a direct impact on your search engine rankings. The major search engines can detect whether or not your website is mobile friendly, and they also know if the potential visitor is searching on their phone. When they search, mobile users are more likely to be suggested mobile-friendly websites.

In Canada, according the Canadian Internet Research Authority (CIRA), 49% of all internet traffic in 2019 was via mobile devices, and according to a 2020 Statista report, that figure is the same in the US. The CIRA report also revealed that 57% of Canadian Boomers are surfing the web on a mobile device — that's more than double the number who were using mobile devices for browsing in 2015.

As I mentioned earlier, it is unlikely and unreasonable that you'll be expected to build a website. However, you absolutely should be armed with the fact above, because of the potential impact it will have on the amount of money you might raise from visitors that come to your website through organic search. This is because an increasing number of online donations come from mobile devices—as many as 1 in every 4 online donations to be precise—based on Blackbaud's most recent Charitable Giving Report (2019). If your website is being buried in search results because it isn't mobile friendly, that's a significant audience of qualified prospects that you're missing out on. And, of those mobile visitors that do land on your homepage, when they find it cumbersome or confusing, there's no way they'll be making it all the way through to your donation form.

As you're creating your blog posts, petitions, landing pages, or donation forms, it's critical that you test them as thoroughly as possible on a variety of phones. Not simply one iPhone and one Android! Test on as many generations of iPhone as you can, as well as Samsung,

Motorola, Nokia, etc. In a past job I had a running list in my head of who in my life had what types of phones so that I could send them a link or email to test. This can be one of the more painful and tedious parts of your job. You get that product looking perfect on your screen and phone, then find out it looks very different on someone else's, which kicks off hours of fiddling and fussing. But the seamless end product will make it well worth the effort.

If none of the above is news to you, then I suggest you look into mobile payment systems, like Google Pay and Apple Pay that offer contactless tap-to-pay functionality if you're processing a transaction in person. Increasingly, the payment options are appearing within mobile phone apps to seamlessly and quickly complete a transaction.

As you may have already noticed, a theme that runs through this small chapter is there are so many ways that you can improve your website's ability to raise money without being a web developer. Armed with the knowledge of what you want to see, and clear rationale as to why, is just what you need to start the process and manage the project in your charity.

3.
EMAIL MARKETING

E mail marketing, put simply, is *the use of an email platform to send a message to a large group of people that have opted-in to communications from your charity.* This is distinctly different from using a website or program (Personal Gmail, Outlook, etc.) to send messages to individuals on behalf of yourself. There are some workarounds and plugins that can help a personal account function like an email marketing platform, but these will rarely be scalable or cost effective if you're looking to reach large groups, integrate with a donor database, and use well-designed email templates.

An underpinning of all great email marketing programs is permission. Without permission from your audience to communicate, you'll be violating one or more anti-SPAM regulations that come with a hefty fine (yes, even if you're a charity), not to mention the fact that you'll erode trust and credibility with the general public. It is well worth brushing up on the regulations within your country, be it the Canadian Anti-Spam Legislation (CASL), General Data Protection Regulation (GDPR), the Controlling the Assault of Non-Solicited Pornography And Marketing Act (CAN-SPAM) in the USA, or the California Consumer Privacy Act (CCPA) in California.

When you hear the term 'opt-in', it is referring to permission from an individual to be sent mass emails from your charity. A sender is only required by law to gain permission once. Ideally you will always collect **explicit permission** from an individual, which could mean they signed up on a clearly marked form, or they clicked an opt-in box for future communications while completing a transaction of some kind, such as entering a contest, or signing an e-petition. **Implicit permission** to contact an individual is at times a valid form of permission, and means that an individual has willingly provided their email address to you but without an explicit request to receive mass email communications. An example of this might be if someone submits the 'Contact Us' form on your website, or they are an active volunteer with an email on file.

Let's break emails down to their most basic elements. These are present in even the most simple emails:

☐ 'From' name and email address

- ☐ 'To' email address
- ☐ 'Reply-to' email address (if not the same as your 'From' email)
- ☐ Subject line
- ☐ Body message, which contains the message you're sending.

In addition to the components listed above, there are additional optional components of an email that can be added:

- ☐ Pre-header text & links (sometimes called *preview text*)
- ☐ Header image or text
- ☐ Body images, links, buttons
- ☐ Social media links/icons
- ☐ Footer, often containing contact info, unsubscribe link, copyrights, etc.

While cooking up your creative copy, designs, and tracking, it is critical that you not lose sight of the many important decisions throughout the email development process that might lower the chances of your email being flagged as SPAM by Gmail, Outlook.com, or another similar email service. The likelihood of an email arriving in an inbox rather than being marked as SPAM is called **deliverability**. Using a trusted and reputable email marketing platform helps tremendously, as well as only sending to a list of people that have provided permission to receive these emails. One way an email service like Gmail might suspect you don't have permission to use a list is by the number of SPAM reports it receives on your emails. But besides these technical considerations, there are some creative and design decisions you can make that will help you avoid those SPAM filters:

- ☐ It should be clear what organization is sending the message.
- ☐ Contact information (email, mailing address, phone) should be included
- ☐ An unsubscribe link should be easy to find, and easy to use.
- ☐ Any images should have a reasonable file size (typically less than 1MB).
- ☐ Avoid special characters (eg !!!, !?) and ALL CAPS in subject lines.
- ☐ Include links to active social media accounts, using icons if possible.
- ☐ Text should be compelling, but brief. Link away to a website if necessary.

A capable and confident digital fundraiser will also employ:

Personalization: This means you are incorporating, when available and possible, biographical information about the recipient. This could include their first and/or last name, and possibly a title if you asked for it. This is usually done using merge fields, where a field from your list is pulled into your email. For example, "Dear %FNAME%," will become "Dear Mary," if done correctly. It is important to note however that each email marketing system will have a different way of inserting a merge field, so please refer to your specific platform's how to's when getting started.

Customization: This means you are matching content, when available and possible, to the recipient's known interests. This could include having a version for cat people, and a version for dog people—information you may have collected when they signed up for your animal shelter email list.

Segmentation: Sending different versions to different groups such as lapsed or new donors.

Timing: Sending on a specific day and/or time.

Link Building: Google provides a simple URL Builder tool that will allow you to encode each individual link within an email with a unique code, called a UTM (Urchin Tracking Module). If you have integrated your donation form with Analytics eCommerce and conversion tracking, this will allow you to see how much money was raised via each link in your email, in addition to clicks. This allows you to gather valuable data about what elements of your email (buttons, body links, images, etc.) are most effective in attracting donations.

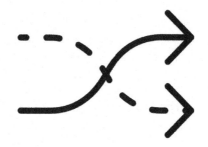

FUNCTION REFORMS
FORM, PERPETUALLY.

Stewart Brand
Long Now Foundation

COMMON EMAIL TYPES

In the course of your digital fundraising career, nearly all of the emails you'll design and send will fit within only a handful of campaign types. There is no universal standard for what these are called, so these are just how I categorize them:

eNewsletters: These emails compile a variety of organizational updates, relevant news, opportunities to volunteer, spotlight donors and supporters, and should be sent consistently on a predictable schedule, such as monthly, bi-weekly, etc. The best eNewsletters are providing real-time updates on your mission with specific examples of progress being made, and the challenges that lie ahead. At the bare minimum, eNewsletters can be an "everything but the kitchen sink" collection of updates that need to be sent—but, remember that even this is better than sending nothing at all.

Your eNewsletters are not going to drive a significant spike in revenue soon after you send. Expect a trickle though! How to attribute this trickle is difficult to pin down, because there are often various messages and opportunities in this single email. A possibility is that the recipient had been meaning to give a donation, and your eNewsletter was the gentle nudge they needed. Great eNewsletters are very effective at developing long-term loyalty.

Promotions & Announcement Emails: These are emails with a single specific piece of information to share, without asking for a donation or action in return. This can be anything from promoting or launching a new partnership (New grant from *The Family Foundation* to do *something great*), announcing an important development (Cancer Research Breakthrough!), to introducing new leadership (Meet *Jane Doe*, our new CEO...).

Engagement Emails: These have a single specific action that you want the recipient to take—typically to donate, pledge, take a survey, or vote. For that reason, let's dig deeper into this email type than we did into eNewsletters or Promotion and Announcement emails. The key with this email type is a *single* specific action. If you find yourself trying to combine more than one 'ask' here, consider reformatting or reverting to the eNewsletter format.

When planning your engagement email campaign, there are questions you should ask yourself at every stage. They are deceptively simple, and it can be easy to lose track. The answer to each is going to direct and reveal your guiding strategy for this specific ask.

1. Who is your audience?
2. What are you asking them to do?
3. Where do they take action?
4. When are you asking them to do it?
5. Why are you asking them?

6. What data or intelligence makes you confident this is the right direction?

With a strategy to guide and maximize your appeal, it's time to plan! Whether working on a single appeal or an annual strategy, it's important to map out the timing (when) and segmentation (who) early in the process, then revisit as necessary. This may only be for your own benefit in which case it doesn't have to be fancy. A Google Sheet may be just fine.

Take the time to learn how to segment within your charity's email platform. A simple and common example of this is when you might want to suppress people that opened the previous email if you're sending a reminder or suppressing recent donors from an appeal. How you do this will vary depending on your platform, and what integrations you may or may not have in place. The most rudimentary way of suppressing a group would be to upload a list for suppression purposes when configuring your list. A more advanced way of doing this would be to have your email marketing platform integrated with your donor database, allowing you to define real-time criteria, or a query, that includes or excludes a segment of your audience.

While you plan out your month or year, I recommend you also sketch out what motivation triggers you might want to test. For example, personal stories, digital advancements, updates from leadership, tax benefits, etc. By doing this you'll be gathering data about what is eliciting a response from your audience, and keeping the content and formats feeling fresh.

Here are some other things to try out, so that you are maximizing engagement within your email program:

→ Within 2-6 days after sending an appeal, send it again with a new subject line to people that **did not** open it the first time around.

→ Isolate people that have not clicked within an email for 6+ months, and have not donated this year. Try out some of your more outlandish design and subject line tests with them. Best case, you reactivate them. Worst case, they unsubscribe which will improve your open and conversion rates on the remaining list.

→ Create and send surveys that uncover donor motivations and behaviours. You can also add fields for additional contact information. Depending on your email platform, you may be able to design the survey in that same platform, which will automatically update the existing account with the new information. Now, you can test them out in your direct mail conversion and prospecting programs.

→ Test out long-form appeals. In direct mail, there are decades of results that show longer letters that are 4-6 pages consistently beat 1-2 page letters. In telefundraising, longer calls also consistently generate a greater ROI than short calls, and one of the most memorable digital fundraising campaigns of the last decade—Kony 2012—was anchored by a 29-minute YouTube documentary.

Automated Emails: Sometimes called "triggered" emails or "drip" emails, these are written once, then sent following a specific action. Some email platforms give customers a tremendous amount of control to create complex workflows that evolve based on actions taken or not taken, and can stretch out for months at a time. A savvy digital fundraiser won't dismiss or undervalue the importance of automated emails. Not only are they a time-saver for charities big and small, these robo-emails are still an opportunity to engage, learn, and educate. The most common automated emails are:

- Donation thank yous, confirmations, e-receipts
- Ticket/purchase confirmations
- Event registration confirmations, tickets and reminders
- Subscribe and unsubscribe confirmations
- New Subscriber welcome series (non-donors)
- New Donor welcome series
- Failed transaction notifications (such as monthly donor card declines)

If you're starting an email program from scratch, start by directing the majority of your time to creating a great multi-step **welcome series**. A basic welcome series typically consists of 2-4 emails over a short period of time, often 2-4 weeks. By sending your welcome series in a timely fashion, you can show sincere gratitude, communicate key information about your charity, and strengthen the bond with this new supporter while their interest in you is fresh and new. When getting started, don't overthink it! It can look as simple as this:

Day 1: Welcome! Here's what you can expect...
Day 6: Come join us on Facebook too!
Day 10: Tell us more about you (short survey)
Day 15: A simple way for you to help... ($ ask)

A simple welcome series is better than no welcome series. Once it is up and running, set a recurring reminder to yourself to check in on the performance of these emails. Do open rates or click-through rates drop drastically from one to the next? Are unsubscribe rates especially high on one or two of them? How many people are converting on that last email? The answers to these questions will guide which changes you make, and why. Think of the four emails as being a funnel, efficiently moving people toward a conversion.

Some (more) Universal Truths About Email: While writing an email—especially a donation appeal—remember that a majority of people read emails in an "F" Pattern, which simply means that they will read most of the first sentence or two, then scan down to the next paragraph and read about half of the first sentence, then skip down to the very end. Take advantage of this user behaviour by ensuring your first sentence is powerful, and pulls readers in. Don't leave your ask to the very end. Instead, try to get an ask in early, then repeat it at the end. Lastly, this pattern reminds us that repetition of a simple key message throughout will maximize the chances that it is seen and engaged with.

In addition to everything covered up to this point, there are a few more best practices for emails that are solely for fundraising purposes:

- ⇢ 'From' name should, if possible, be a person's name that the recipient will recognize. If the name may not yet be familiar to the recipient, include the charity name, like this: *Brock W., Charity ABC*

- ⇢ If you're going to send the email as an individual rather than an organization, the email should be in first person and reflect the writer's voice. If at all possible, include their name in a signature block and a photo of the person and/or an electronic signature.

- ⇢ Images, if used, should complement rather than distract.

- ⇢ A linked donation form should, if possible, match the email branding.

If you're interested in knowing how well your emails are performing compared to others in your sector— great! Being curious about performance is a healthy habit, but my advice is to take any benchmark you might find online with a grain of salt. Benchmarks vary greatly by list size, timing, content, organization type, and brand recognition. A much better use of your time and effort would be to measure and track the metrics that are most meaningful to you. A solid starting point is to track open rates, unsubscribe rate, rate of conversion to a donation, your donation revenue, and average gift amount. Set specific goals for continual improvement, and if you're at a loss as to where to start, M+R produce an incredibly thorough—and free—annual benchmarking report that is a consistently good read to keep you abreast of trends and innovations in email marketing.

Testing: If at all possible within your email marketing platform, test, test, test! Testing is a valuable tool for understanding what is working with your subscribers. The four most common email marketing tests are:

1. Subject Lines
2. 'From' Name
3. Content Variation (e.g., layouts, images, stories, etc)
4. Timing

Email platforms are rapidly improving and simplifying testing for users like you, because the better you are at sending emails, the better results you'll get, which in turn will increase what you invest in your email program. Testing is no longer a nice-to-have feature, and ease of testing and analysis is a feature you should explore thoroughly when considering your first—or your next—email marketing platform.

Some testing advice: only test one variable at a time to ensure your test is as 'clean' as possible. Be mindful of statistical significance measures—the likelihood that the results of a test are real and repeatable, and not just due to chance. The score can be calculated as a Confidence Score, and there are plenty of free online calculators for doing this. Using a system like this will help to keep you honest when assessing test results. For example, a confidence score of 95% or higher will tell you that the results are statistically significant. 75-94% means you should re-test when possible, and under 75% means the results were not statistically significant.

Even if your email marketing platform has user-friendly testing capabilities, be sure to dig deeper into what else may be happening. Let's look at an example of why you should be careful to jump too quickly to declaring a "winner" in an email test:

A charity runs an A/B subject line test to 20% of their 300,000 subscribers, which means 30,000 will get subject line A, and 30,000 receive subject line B. The email version with the most opens after 6 hours will automatically be sent to the remaining 240,000 subscribers.

Subject line A has an open rate of 21% (6,300 opened)
Subject line B has an open rate of 20% (6,000 opened)

Because subject line A had the most opens, it was sent to the balance of the list. But what if subject line B had a click-through rate of 3% versus subject line A's 1%?

> *(A) 1% of 30,000 = 300 clicks*
> *(B) 3% of 30,000 = 900 clicks*

The Confidence Score of the above results is 99%, meaning there is a very high likelihood that you could see these results repeated if this charity were to roll out subject line B—the 'loser' of the test—to the remainder of the list. In this scenario, the version that uses subject line B would have generated 9,300 clicks, whereas subject line A would have only generated 3,900.

Now, let's assume this charity knows from past campaign data that on average, out of everyone who opens an email, 3% give a donation. And, let's assume they know that their average online donation is $172.

> *Email A - [(3,900 opens) x 3%] x $172 = $20,124*
> *Email B - [(9,300 opens) x 3%] x $172 = $47,988*

That's a difference of $27,864 that this charity just missed out on, because of a hasty decision to declare a winner. In all but the largest charities, $27,864 would be considered a major gift if it came in a lump sum, right?

Integrating Email with Direct Mail: Direct mail is still a workhorse for many large and mid-sized charities. It is acquiring new donors cost-effectively, and for donors that have been giving by mail for decades, it is still a preferred method of communicating. Email is a great way to complement and boost your direct mail program—and vice versa. Avoid the temptation to assume that anyone who replies to mail is a Luddite! They very likely use email, social media, text and more—it's just not their preferred method of sending in their donation information.

Digital channels—email in particular—are a great way to emphasize urgency, and give a reminder of how valuable a donor's support is to your charity. Here are a few simple ways you can integrate your direct mail with email to boost your overall returns:

⇢ An email **teaser**, sent just before mail is scheduled to arrive. This can be a *"keep an eye on your mailbox"*-type message on the day that your mail campaign is delivered to the postal service, which means most households will receive your email within a few days.

⇢ An email **followup**, sent just after most mail is received. If you've seeded the mailing with your address, send this email 3-5 business days after that seed arrives. This can be a *"did you get our letter?"* message.

The most effective tactic is to do both. If your email platform and your database are synced up with an integration, you will just have to isolate the mail recipients with a query or condition. If your email platform and database are not linked with an integration, then the low-tech way would be to export email addresses as a field when pulling your mailing list. You'll then be able to upload these contacts into your email platform as a unique audience.

Integrating Email with Digital Ads and Social Media: For any email appeal you send, it would be wise to create a custom donation form specific to your appeal. Most donation processing platforms make this as quick and easy as copying an existing form, then changing a label or field in the administrator platform so that you can isolate donations received through this specific form. Before you post on social media about your appeal, you can use Google's URL Builder tool to create a unique URL for tracking clicks and other user behaviours in Google Analytics. While in there, you will also be able to identify how much traffic— commonly called 'referrals'—this form receives from various social media channels.

If you have a budget for paid social media advertising, you can use that same email list that you just exported from your database to create a custom audience in Facebook Business Manager, or the Google Adwords Platform. You can then design and display advertising to those people—provided that the email address you have on file is the same email address they use for their social media account—to reinforce your appeal messaging, and possibly give people that reminder they need to give their gift.

Mobile Optimization: It would be wise to assume that the first glance at your email will be on a phone, which means there are some specific copywriting and design considerations. All that someone might see of your subject line could be 3-4 words before it is abbreviated. You'll want to avoid an email that is just one large static image with a lot of small text. These can be difficult to read once shrunk down to the size of a screen, and unless you have all of that text in a plain-text version of the email, the message cannot be accessed by anyone that might be using an assistive device.

4.
ANALYTICS

W e've mentioned Google Analytics several times up to this point in the book. If you've skipped ahead to this section—welcome! Like several of the chapters in this book, analyzing website traffic and behaviours is an immense topic. What we are going to do here is attempt to establish a baseline understanding of what Google Analytics is, what it can be used for, and why that is important for your digital fundraising program.

What we won't be doing here in this chapter is a comprehensive *How To* guide, because Google provides extensive and thorough (and free) training on how to become an Analytics whiz in their Analytics Academy. The features of Analytics are also constantly evolving, along with the user interface, which means this book would be outdated or inaccurate within months of publishing. Google also provides great customer service, along with an active community of people willing to help in official support forums. I highly recommend you take advantage of these services if you're having trouble with the Analytics platform before you begin calling a consultant or agency. Third-party experts are best used for bespoke, customized work you may want developed that would fall outside typical Google support services.

Google Analytics is a powerful, free platform for measuring a wide variety of activities and behaviours of visitors to your charity's website. When you set up a free account, you are provided with a Universal Analytics (UA) number that is unique to your webpage. Google provides a few lines of code—called a 'snippet'—that needs to be added to the code of your website, along with a few ways to then verify that the code has been installed correctly. From that point forward, Google Analytics will be active. Don't be put off by the idea of inserting code; many website building platforms simplify the process where you may not need to do more than simply entering your UA number into a single field.

It is often easy and always wise to connect your other platforms and properties to your Google Analytics account. This can include your official social media accounts, email marketing platform, and certainly all other Google tools you might be using, like YouTube, Adwords, Search Console or Tag Manager. Linking these together with a single UA code helps to verify and track the behaviours of visitors that have left one website for another, which is what Google calls cross-domain tracking.

If you've never seen or interacted with the Google Analytics platform, it is important to note here that what you'll see in your dashboard is aggregate, anonymized information about visitor behaviour. While you can see a tremendous amount of information about what someone has been up to on your site, you can not identify exactly who that visitor is. With enough data, you can also drill down into what age brackets your visitors fit into, some of their other interests and shopping habits, gender, etc. As a fundraiser, this information can be helpful data to bring into sponsorship proposals, where the business would appreciate knowing that there is an alignment between your charity's audience and their target purchaser demographic.

Being the savvy digital fundraiser that you are, if you take nothing else away from this section, let it be that *unless your charity configures the ability to track donation conversions, then Google Analytics is not going to help you raise any additional online revenue*. By configuring **eCommerce tracking** in Google Analytics, your donation platform will report back to Google Analytics the value of the final transaction. You won't know that Jane Doe gave $300—but, you will know that a visitor who clicked a link on social media then came to your website and completed a $300 donation. This type of information is critically important data for guiding your strategies, and for optimization of future campaigns. Data and statistics about visits, clicks, and bounce rates are nice to know as well.

GOOGLE TAG MANAGER

In the course of your Analytics education, you'll no doubt see and hear about Google Tag Manager (GTM) as a great addition to your web analytics toolkit—and it is! But, it's more advanced than your basic suite of tools and reports in Google Analytics, and may not be the best place to start. GTM offers website administrators, marketers and digital fundraisers like yourself more control over the array of 'tags' that they are adding to their website code. As your digital fundraising program matures, and your tracking, reporting and analysis needs expand, I recommend you install GTM and take advantage of the free training resources that Google offers.

GOALS AND CONVERSIONS

In Google Analytics, you have the ability to define what qualifies as a conversion, and set specific goals for what you believe is an accurate measure of success. A conversion does not necessarily mean a donation. A conversion can be anything from a visitor signing up for your eNewsletter, watching an embedded video, or downloading an app. If you aren't defining and reporting on conversions and goals yourself, I strongly recommend that you always clarify what someone is referring to when they report on a conversion.

Speaking from experience, it's possible that what you value as a meaningful conversion may not be shared by your non-fundraiser teammates, because digital fundraising is not their primary focus or area of expertise. For example, let's say you are running advertisements on social media to sell tickets for your upcoming golf tournament fundraiser. There should be no more important metric in this campaign than the number of tickets sold, because from those two numbers we can calculate our advertising ROI. A shockingly common mistake I see made by small and mid-sized charities is that they will invest in advertising campaigns just like this, but without setting up conversion tracking that extends all the way to the final transaction. Impressions, engagements, visits, and clicks are often much more impressive numbers on the surface, but if the purpose of your campaign is to raise money, they are largely vanity metrics.

5.
ONLINE ADVERTISING

W hile they're far from being as flashy as billboards or guerilla marketing, **search engine marketing** (SEM) and **search engine optimization** (SEO) are workhorses of the digital advertising ecosystem. While they share similar names because of the space they occupy, they are in fact quite different. SEO refers essentially to deliberate strategies and tactics to improve your website's search engine rankings, which should in turn bring you closer to the top of the search results when your charity and its programming are relevant. The higher you rank, the more traffic you'll get. SEM refers to the practice of designing and targeting ads to people that—hopefully—want to buy what you're selling. In your case, it's a charitable cause.

Fair warning: if you were to try to do everything outlined in this chapter, it would be a full-time job and then some. For good reason, there are agencies and freelancers that specialize in this work, so if you are strapped for time, but desire to add one of these tactics to your digital fundraising mix, I recommend testing the market for freelance support. The dedicated attention and expertise will really help jumpstart this area of your program.

Search Engine Marketing and Digital Advertising: Unlike traditional mass media (TV, radio, outdoor, etc.), digital advertising offers the ability for advertisers—in this case, you—to target very specific audiences of people online, and to set specific parameters over how your money is spent. Digital advertising is <u>not</u> a niche tactic.

In 2017, spending (in the US) on digital advertising surpassed TV for the first time in history, making it the top target for advertising dollars. Why? Because when done properly, digital advertising gives advertisers far more confidence that their investments are generating the expected returns, as compared to tactics like outdoor ads (billboards, posters, etc.), television, or radio. Take this scenario for example:

A fundraising manager wants to acquire 3,000 new email subscribers. They have a budget of $3,000 for this project. With this, they could create a great poster which is displayed in 3 subway stations for 1 month. Or, they could run a Facebook ad campaign for email signups, with a budget of $1 per email signup, and a maximum spend of $3,000.

Those subway advertisements in that example could greatly exceed expectations, or just as likely, they could woefully underperform. Either way, the $3,000 budget has been spent. In the Facebook scenario, the campaign will only spend the full $3,000 if the goal of 3,000 subscribers is achieved.

Digital Advertising is a catch-all term that includes a variety of tactics for reaching potential donors and customers online.

1. Paid Search

These are text-only ads that appear at the top of the search results for specific keywords or phrases. They will often look very similar to the other organic search results that you are given.

2. Display Advertisements

These are images designed in a variety of dimensions and file formats that appear within websites or within mobile apps. These are simple, but effective. While the ads tend to appear in a handful of sizes (banner, big box, skyscraper, etc.), there are in fact dozens more dimensions that can be used, from very small banners for mobile apps up to super-sized banners for high-resolution 4K monitors.

3. Paid Social

Advertisers can choose from a wide variety of content formats that are served to specific audiences of people. This can range from "boosting" the reach of a basic post or article, promoting a video, email signups, petitions, "Story" posts, etc.

4. Video (pre-roll or mid-roll)

These are the short commercials that you might see before (pre-roll) or during (mid-roll) a YouTube video, and which you are sometimes able to skip. This tactic also pops up on websites that host their own video within their website, such as news channels or TV stations. If you've noticed a short video ad appear in your Instagram stories, that is called an interstitial.

5. Affiliate Links/Influencer Marketing

Although affiliate links are somewhat less common for nonprofits, it's worth knowing how they work. Essentially, individuals or small companies can earn a small commission on a product that is sold online, provided the purchaser came via a unique URL. This is very common amongst bloggers. A different way of achieving a similar outcome is with unique promo codes—if you enter a specific promo code, you may unlock a small discount for yourself, but you *may* also be earning a small commission for the person who provided you that promo code.

6. Branded Content

With podcasts and video content being consumed online more than ever before, there is a surge in this form of advertising. Essentially, advertisers are underwriting the costs of producing professional content, which could be a podcast episode or series, or a YouTube video that relates somewhat to the product or service you are promoting, but without being an outright advertisement. It's subtle—rather than paying to advertise on someone else's show or channel, the advertisers are commissioning it to be made from scratch. A hypothetical but possible example of this could be if Rapala (the fishing lure company) commissioned a four-part podcast series about the history of bass fishing, called *Gettin' Jiggy With It*. Anglers would love it, and Rapala would have exclusive advertising rights.

While there are clearly many, many channels and tactics to employ, there are some fundamentals in digital advertising that won't change. **A great digital advertisement is specific, relevant, attractive, and empowering.** With this in mind, next it's important to define some specific and tangible goals, and to ensure you have alignment with your team or managers on your goals at the outset of a campaign. Google's advertising platform categorizes goals into six distinct actions that you could want someone to take. While this is Google's list, it's a solid foundation for whichever platform you might be using.

1. Buy something online: clothing, books, or just give a donation.
2. Visit a website: your homepage, a campaign landing page, or a specific news article or blog post.

3. Take an action on a website: fill out a form, survey, pledge.

4. Call: to learn more about your charity's programs or services, or to donate.

5. See an ad: promoting your awareness or brand campaign.

6. Visit a location: your museum, classes, library, or another site you might have.

Within the six goals listed above—as well as others that may emerge in years to come—you can further home in on exactly how you want to focus your investment to achieve that goal. This is your bidding strategy, which is named as such because what it costs to have your ad displayed alongside a keyword or phrase is constantly fluctuating based on supply and demand. Bid strategies can include:

1. **Manual Bidding:** This bidding strategy means you manually set a price that you believe a given campaign, advertisement or keyword is worth to you. By setting a cost per click (CPC) upper limit, you may have peace of mind that you're not overpaying for a keyword. This hands-on approach is much more time consuming than an automated bidding strategy, unless you have a very small, simple and targeted campaign you are running. In the hands of an expert though, manual bidding can be very effective.

2. **Automated Bidding:** This bidding strategy will employ a variety of machine learning—or

artificial intelligence (AI)—to adjust the amount you pay per click depending on demand at the given time. You can set your daily budget, so while the cost per click (CPC) may fluctuate greatly throughout the day, you can be certain that you won't exceed your daily budget. If you choose to employ automatic bidding, you can further instruct the AI to focus on what might be of most importance to you in your campaign.

BONUS: Smart Bidding: If manual and automatic bidding were to form a Venn diagram, Smart Bidding would form the overlap in the middle, because it is an optional strategy that can be applied to manual or automatic bidding strategies. Think of this as a constellation of strategies that are being deployed simultaneously to give you the best return on your advertising investment. Google will balance measures like Cost per Action (CPA), Return on Ad Spend (ROAS), maximizing conversion, maximizing conversion value, and "enhanced" cost per click (ECPC). If you're choosing to use an automated bid strategy, you will need to make some more decisions—namely, choosing how you would like the automated system to prioritize your spend:

a. **Focusing on Conversions:** Rather than solely focusing on clicks which only tells you that the person clicked your ad, a focus on conversions goes further and optimizes spend on the potential donors that are most likely to convert into donors, email subscribers, etc. This will require you to link Google Analytics or a tracking pixel with the advertising platform. You can choose to also prioritize spending on the value of conversions, rather than a binary yes/no conversion outcome. Google also uses the term and acronym Return on Ad Spend (ROAS) which is the value of the conversion (the value of the donation) compared to the amount spent to acquire it to determine the ROAS.

b. **Focusing on Impressions:** This strategy is more common on social media than in search engines, and will attempt to display (or commonly called 'serve') your ad to as many people as possible, which might mean that in doing so, the ad won't be shown to the top-tier prospects. This will mean lots of people see your ad, but not as many clicks. If you're looking to simply get your name out there, this is one way to do this.

c. **Focusing on Website Visits:** This is good for targeted campaigns where you are less concerned about a specific conversion (such as a donation or email signup), and instead you just want people to visit your website. In doing so they may learn more about your cause, and you may be able to target them for advertising in the future.

d. **Focus on Video Views and/or Conversions:** If you've made the investment of time and money into creating a fantastic piece of video, you would be wise to want to have it suggested or served to likely potential donors. YouTube and Facebook are littered with great videos that were uploaded with no plan or strategy for increasing views. With the correct tracking code or pixels on your website, it is possible to track and optimize for people who eventually converted after having watched your promoted video.

SEARCH ENGINE OPTIMIZATION

All search engines, most notably Google, are regularly updating the ways in which they score and rank websites. It is very much a moving target. The primary reason these companies are regularly evolving their algorithm is so that they can continue to serve up the most relevant search results to users as possible. A secondary reason is that with each new release, there are website administrators out there that find ways to exploit the new algorithm to their advantage, and in ways it was not intended. This results in a lower quality of search results, and the cycle repeats.

Trying to stay abreast of the latest SEO tactics and algorithm updates is a full-time job. To get the biggest bang for your buck, there are some fundamentals that if you do well, will set your charity up for success:

Search engines will always be seeking out websites that are kept up to date, because who wants to be sent to a website whose last news article was published over a year ago? Search engines can also determine—whether you tell it this or not—what your primary purpose or product is, and how authoritative you are on the topic. One simple way this is done is with keywords. You don't need to be overly clever here. If you support sickle cell disease patients in Vancouver, then your core 3–5 keywords will likely revolve around those facts. They might look like:

Sickle Cell Disease Patient Support
Sickle Cell Disease Charities
Sickle Cell Charity
Sickle Cell Disease Vancouver
Sickle Cell Anemia Vancouver

If the main pages on your website—typically About Us, Programs, Volunteer, Contact and Donate—are reinforcing that this is a page about these topics, then you'll be well on your way. If you've linked your Google Analytics code to your website code, as well as your social media pages, then you'll be maximizing the chances that Google appends and recognizes the correct accounts as people search.

The majority of websites these days—or at least the administrative sections that you will be using—make the changing of basic website content pretty straightforward. Changing text, selecting from some pre-designed templates, and adding photo or video shouldn't require you to know how to write or edit code.

If you've been inside a text editor for a website, you'll have seen some familiar functions for changing your text size and other formatting functions. These are often called a "WYSIWYG" (pronounced whiz-ee-wig) which is an acronym for *What You See Is What You Get*. A feature in there is to style your text with pre-defined formatting for Header 1, Header 2, Subheading, Body, and so on. A benefit of using these pre-defined styles, rather than just manipulating the text directly, is that search engines can use these style tags as information about what this page is about, and what text is more important than others.

GOOGLE ADWORDS GRANT

Google offers a suite of services and tools to nonprofits through their *Google for Nonprofits* program. If accepted into this program, charities can apply for an Adwords grant which provides up to $10,000/month in advertising credit. It is limited to text ads on Google, and your ads will appear below the ads of paid advertisements. Adwords grants are great for increasing visibility online. Directly, they don't raise much money for most charities using them. They can collect new subscribers, followers, or page likes, and therefore potential future donors. To get your account up and running, and to keep it active, Google sets some minimum standards, such as having at least a 5% clickthrough rate (CTR) as an average across your account, and they require you to have conversion tracking set up so that smart bidding can be utilized. Requirements such as this do change, so be sure to stay up to date on the latest recommendations and make the necessary changes, or risk your grant being revoked.

I'm often asked if the Adwords Grant is worth the time and effort, and the answer truly is, it depends. If you're the only fundraiser in your organization, then no, your time would be better spent elsewhere. But it can be a great project for a junior staff member, a summer intern, or a tech-savvy volunteer.

6.
(MORE) TESTING

D otted throughout nearly every chapter of this book is a reference to testing, measurement and tracking. That's for good reason! The adage "If you can't measure it, you can't track it" is true, but it's also easier said than done. Each tool and platform varies somewhat in the metrics they provide, what they call them, and how you can view them.

If you want to test something, you have to know how to measure that thing. A fundamental to understand is that nearly all metrics (or measurements) can be slotted into one of three categories, each representing a stage within a funnel-shaped path to conversion.

1. **Awareness**: This is the top of your funnel, and is the category of metrics that represent how many people may have seen your post or advertisement. This category often gives you the biggest numbers because of how broadly it can be applied. For example, if your charity has 500

Twitter followers and you tweet a photo from your gala, and one of the attendees who has 5,000 followers retweets that photo, then the original tweet now has now reached 5,500 users. While at face value that is true and might sound impressive, the reality is that only a fraction of those 5,500 users would have seen the tweet. Some people may not use Twitter anymore, some may not have been logged on, and even if someone saw it, they may have just kept scrolling. Awareness metrics on their own are just vanity metrics, because they only tell a very small part of a very large story. Their power is truly unlocked when you begin combining them with engagement and conversion metrics to calculate and forecast a much more actionable use case. Reach is often reported as a specific type of metric, which is the number of people that you can be certain saw your post. Impressions are similar but refers to the number of times it was seen, which means it can attribute multiple views to a single person.

2. **Engagement**: This is the middle of your funnel, and is where we slot in the many different actions that a visitor, follower, or subscriber might take. While the number of people that make it to the middle of the funnel decreases, the complexity is going to ramp up quite quickly. It's in this part of the funnel where you'll keep the data about what people are doing with your offers (subscribing to your email list,

downloading a report, signing a petition, etc.). It's also where you might slot in the many different actions that your email subscribers can take, including open, click-through rates, and unsubscribe rates.

3. **Conversion**: The bottom of the funnel is where you keep your most valuable actions. Donations will certainly be in here, and you can drill further down into those metrics for actions like converted visitors into new donors, lapsed donors into active donors, new or upgraded monthly donors, etc. To accurately measure at this stage of the funnel, you'll need to be sure you have as many conversion-tracking pixels and snippets in place as possible.

These three funnel stages are just a starting point for creating and customizing a measurement framework that works for you. There are dozens—if not hundreds—of different funnel examples readily available online that can suit different channel mixes and offer types.

As you're planning out what your funnel(s) will look like, it can often be helpful to work from the bottom up, starting with the outcome you want to see, then working backwards identifying what would have to take place for this to happen. For example, you can start with the bottom of the funnel conversion goal of new monthly donors, then begin developing possible use cases about what type of actions people may have taken before signing up as a monthly donor. These hypotheses begin to look like:

How likely is someone to sign up as a monthly donor if they…

- ⇢ Complete an online survey?

- ⇢ Have given a one-time gift online in the last year?

- ⇢ Sign up to volunteer?

- ⇢ Subscribed to our email list?

- ⇢ Receive a text message?

Each of the above actions is packed with some assumptions that you'll need to consider and try to account or control for. For example, for someone to complete an online survey sent via email, you'd have to have their email address and permission to contact them. To send a text message, you would need to have been provided their cell phone number and permission to contact. How did you get those emails and phone numbers? Questions like this form the next level up in your funnel, and they spider all the way up to variations on the question of "How did they hear about us?"

If the sheer number of possibilities for funnels and pathways has you feeling overwhelmed, my advice is to keep laser-focused on the most meaningful conversions that you need or want to know, *and* that you can measure with existing digital tools. You will also find them an especially helpful tool within specific digital campaigns because they will help you isolate specific strengths or weaknesses that you can address quickly to improve results. Here's an example of what that might look like for a basic lead generation campaign:

> *Charity A wants to acquire new monthly donors by creating a petition that will be promoted on social media. The petition will be on a landing page with tracking cookies, and will require a name and email, with an optional field for their phone number. The reach and impressions of these advertisements are the top of funnel metrics.*

> *If someone clicks through and is on the landing page, there are three possibilities: they fill out the entire form, they provide name and email, but not phone, or they leave without doing anything. Each of these are valuable middle of funnel data points.*

> *Next you'll put anyone who provided a phone number into a telefundraising stream, the email-only contacts get an email appeal, and the people who left are targeted again with digital ads by using remarketing (retargeting). The successful conversions here form your conversion metrics at the bottom of your funnel.*

Specific appeals and test cases like this are where you can really put the funnel to good use. If you see that telefundraising is converting really well, you might opt to make the phone number field mandatory at signup. You'll have fewer total signups, but you will increase the number of new monthly donors

SECTION III:
BUILD IT

Now that you're equipped with a solid understanding of digital fundraising's core concepts, it's time that we start stitching them together into the more recognizable and outward facing campaigns, appeals and communications that the public and your donors will fall in love with.

On top of those slow-moving layers that we covered in Sections I and II, this section is when we rise out into the shiny, fast-moving layers that get the lion's share of attention and adoration. This is also the layer of your digital program where the thoughtful decisions about technological infrastructure and creative risks fuse together.

This section focuses on high-level strategy and execution, in a largely platform-agnostic manner. What may or may not be possible within one charity's set of platforms will vary greatly amongst the readers of this book, which prevents me as your guide from giving the step-by-step instructions we all want. In other words, expect far more 'what' and 'why' than 'how' in this section. But, if I've done my job well you should have enough of an understanding of, and vocabulary for, designing highly effective digital fundraising campaigns and appeals.

1.
CAMPAIGNS AND APPEALS

The term *campaign* is a particularly slippery one in our nonprofit space, and fundraisers are guilty of throwing the term around a lot. To be sure we're aligned throughout this chapter, let's take a moment to establish clarity here.

Do any of these sound familiar?

Capital campaign
Bequest, Legacy or Planned Giving campaign
Stewardship campaign
Annual campaign
Comprehensive campaign

Integrated campaign
Multichannel campaign
Membership campaign
Renewal campaign
Awareness campaign

And so it goes, ad nauseam. Let's use this basic definition of a campaign, and build on it as we move forward: *digital fundraising **campaigns** are a consistent, measurable effort to raise funds for the needs of the charity from a specific constituency.* The term is also often used interchangeably—sometimes accurately, sometimes not—with the appeals, tactics, segments, and offers that are being used to bring your campaign to life. Below is a basic hierarchy of how a college or university might structure a fundraising coding structure, from the broad down to the granular and specific. The benefit of this basic framework as a starting point is that when used consistently, it can provide plenty of flexibility in how you can report back on results, and analyze those results for new opportunities.

Funds
(Annual Fund, Capital Fund, Endowment Fund etc.)

⇓

Campaigns
(Membership, Monthly Giving, Mid-Level, etc.)

⇓

Appeals
(Year-end, Emergency, Monthly Conversion, etc.)

⇓

Tactics
(Mail, Online, etc.)

⇓

Segments and Tests
(A/B tests, versioning, etc.)

Here is an example of how this might look in actual practice:

Janice Doe just gave $50 to your latest email appeal to support scholarship opportunities before school starts in the fall.

Fund: Scholarship Fund
Campaign: Annual Giving (one-time gifts < $500)
Appeal: 2020 Summer Renewal Ask
Tactic: Email
Segment: Alumni
Test: First name personalization in subject line

In this example, you can see how you might be able to analyze and report in dozens of different ways. Your finance department will be able to easily recognize the Scholarship Fund bank accounts with database entries, leadership can report to the board of directors on the overall success of the summer renewal efforts, and your communications team will be interested to know how actively the alumni base is—or is not—responding to appeals.

As a front-line digital fundraiser, you'll have far more control over and vested interest in appeals. In Section I we outlined the many types of emails you'll use within an email marketing program, but not all were specific to fundraising and organizing. There are six primary types of digital fundraising appeals—meaning there is a single, specific call to action—that will dominate the majority of your fundraising appeal calendar.

1. Year-end Appeals
2. Emergency Appeals
3. Peer-to-Peer (P2P) Fundraising
4. Advocacy/Lead Generation
5. Stewardship
6. Crowdfunding

YEAR-END APPEALS

A year-end fundraising appeal for most charities is their most successful digital appeal. The looming deadline to receive a charitable gift receipt is a factor, but it is only one amongst many motivators, and is unlikely the leader. I believe it is often so successful because it is one of the few—if not only—times that many charities deliver a clear and "hard" ask for a gift, along with a deadline. Specific, urgent, and time-bound. These are qualities that we shouldn't hide in storage ten months a year like pumpkin spice and Michael Bublé.

These appeals should have multiple sequenced components spread out over an 8-12 week period. My advice is typically to be fully prepared and ready to launch just after (Canadian) Thanksgiving in mid-October. This amount of time may feel too long to some, but it will provide enough space to employ a variety of tools, tactics, and variation to encourage donations before December 31st.

The best year-end appeals:

Have a consistent theme that ties together the various stories you'll employ for your asks and reminders.

Have a distinct visual identity within your brand guidelines so that donors develop a near-instant association with this identity, this specific appeal, and your charity.

Escalate in urgency as the December 31st deadline approaches.

Make a compelling case for giving NOW. Any hints or suggestions that a gift can wait for another time will undermine the urgency and need you have established. If someone is unable or unwilling to give, they won't, and that's fine!

Segment communications to ensure the most relevant ask is being made, thus increasing your success rate. This can include segmenting and customizing for lapsed donors, recent donors, monthly donors, alumni, regional variances, etc.

Suppress responders as they give, so that no one is being asked for a gift within days or weeks of having just given.

Become the focal point of the charity's communications and marketing for a defined window of time, reinforcing the importance and urgency of this appeal for help.

Celebrate and showcase donor generosity and impact, whether en masse in some way, or with direct and personal followups.

Common year end appeal mistakes:

Not emailing enough. If you include each segment and consider that the later stage emails will be going to your most non-responsive subscribers, 10 or more emails in a 12-week period would not be unreasonable.

Don't email on Dec. 30 and/or Dec. 31. While there is some lively debate amongst fundraisers about how donor-centric a December 31st email is, I feel strongly that these emails can be written tastefully, and if you don't send them, you're leaving money on the table.

Use budget shortfalls as a case for giving rather than staying focused on the needs of your beneficiaries, and the impact of donations on making the world a better place.

Feel repetitive by recycling content, signatories, quotes, stories or images. As you notice a significant dip in open rates and clickthrough rates, it's time to pull out some fresh names, layouts, or subject lines.

Don't customize a landing page or donation form to match the appeal, which can leave the donor wondering if they've arrived in the right place.

Failing to customize acknowledgements to the campaign. It shouldn't add more than a few hours' work to revisit your standard thank you letter and/or email acknowledgement.

Lack of integration between channels, especially with direct mail, social media, and telefundraising. The planning and preparation to ensure all these parts are moving in synchrony is a challenge, but often results in significantly higher returns.

EMERGENCY APPEALS

An emergency appeal, or sometimes called a "special" appeal, is an ask to support a specific project or need, which requires asking for support over and above a donor's typical level or timing of giving. An example of this would be a humanitarian aid charity asking their active monthly donors for a single gift to support their response to an earthquake.

When the need truly is urgent, and especially when the emergency or topic is in the news, these appeals are incredibly effective. When you have this swell of support on your side, move as quickly as possible. You'll raise much more money, and your donors will be proud to support an organization that is nimble and responsive.

The best emergency appeals:

Are timely. A 2016 study by Colin Habberton of Relativ Group based in South Africa unpacked the speed at which public discussion moves on from one crisis to the next on social media, and found that within 48 hours of a crisis, the volume of conversation about a topic will have returned to normal. Your window of opportunity is incredibly small, so don't miss it.

Acknowledge current or recent gifts, and loyalty which should happen early in the copy or script so that it's not overlooked by the donor.

Clearly state why they are asking, and the impact so that even if a donor is unable or unwilling to donate, they should at least feel that the act of asking was justified.

Are, when possible, not conflicting with ongoing appeals. In the case of natural disasters, you can't predict the future. However, there are times when you can anticipate a spike in a need for resources, such as an upcoming election, rainy seasons where there are dense refugee populations, or seniors struggling with isolation and heating bills.

Are unapologetic about asking. If you're unsure whether or not the timing is right, it probably isn't. There's a good chance your donor might be just as skeptical about the timing and need.

Keep donors updated on progress and impact.
Whether your emergency appeal is a success or not,
make a point to inform donors on this appeal as
soon as you're able with an update on how their gift
was used and the impact it's having.

Common emergency appeal mistakes:

A soft ask which undermines the urgency your
appeal needs to be successful. This is not the time to
ask for a gift that's *"less than a cup of coffee a day,"*
or *"whatever you can manage."*

Including more than one financial call to action. In
my experience, adding a non-financial ask—such as
asking the public to email their member of
Parliament, or sign a petition—as a secondary
option to giving a donation will not suppress your
overall results. Avoid combining one-time and
monthly asks, or mixing in promotions for your
upcoming event.

**Lack of support on social media which undermines
urgency**. Many digital native donors, especially
those who may be just learning about your charity,
will check out social media pages as part of their
research and vetting. The emergency appeal should
be pinned to your profile.

PUBLIC OUTCRY IS MOST
PRONOUNCED 24HRS AFTER AN
EVENT. KNOWING WHEN THIS
MOMENT OCCURS CAN HELP
BETTER LEVERAGE THIS OUTCRY
FOR CHANGE.

Colin Habberton
Relativ Group

PEER-TO-PEER (P2P) APPEALS

While you may only associate P2P fundraising with mega-events like bike rides across the country or running marathons, they are more accurately defined broadly as *any fundraising appeals that are designed to utilize the personal networks of your donors, empowering them to fundraise on your behalf.* There is always some implicit hope that our donors will power a word of mouth campaign that might in turn attract more donors. A P2P appeal turns that implicit hope into an explicit ask.

Three common types of P2P efforts are:

1. **Group Activity**: A group of people are going to gather (in person or virtually) for some sort of activity or event. This includes walkathons, bike rides, colour runs, etc.

2. **Individual Event/Challenge**: Someone sets a personal goal, or celebrates a personal milestone and links it to a fundraising target. Think of birthdays, mountain climbing, moustache growing, or anything else that our creative supporters can dream up.

3. **Personal Fundraising**: An individual sets a personal fundraising goal linked to impact, but it is not connected to an event or milestone. Examples might include raising money for medical research because they are personally

affected, or rallying support for a workplace United Way campaign.

The best P2P campaigns (regardless of type):

Encourage the organizer to give the first gift, to set the tone. The social proof of having one or more donations on a personal fundraising page is incredibly powerful when your potential donor arrives. It also shows friends and family that they are not asking for something that they aren't willing to do themselves.

Clearly communicate the impact of a gift throughout the duration of the appeal. Don't lose the thread of what impact and outcomes this fundraising will generate.

Develop a sense of community when there is a group effort underway, by gathering stories and sharing them back to the larger group. Call your top fundraisers to thank them and learn more about their story, and with their permission you can write and publish a profile about them.

Incentivize fundraising, where appropriate and applicable. In some scenarios this could be an early bird deadline for event registrations, or a special gift for the first 50 people to hit their fundraising goal.

Create and share fundraising guides, tips and tools. There often comes a point when P2P fundraisers lose momentum and are positive that they've tried everything. A succinct fundraising guide, whether interactive or downloadable as a

PDF, can give them the fresh ideas they need to hit their goal.

Nudge or remind inactive fundraisers as deadlines approach. Don't be quick to assume that an inactive fundraiser is anything but busy, and has every intention to get around to sending their first appeal emails.

Thank and welcome new donors right away, and acknowledge the source. You may have some technical limitations here, but within a growing number of P2P platforms you can customize your automated emails to acknowledge the name of the participant that this donor has sponsored. These small touches do add up!

Report back to everyone involved on the impact of the gift. If you've invested all this time into building community, rallying and cheerleading, don't let it fizzle out. Be sure to let everyone involved—organizers, volunteers, donors, and sponsors—what incredible work they helped make possible.

Common P2P appeal mistakes (regardless of type):

Don't emphasize the importance of email for fundraising. While social media gets all the attention, email still has all the power. When coaching your organizers, make sure that your top tip is to start with a personal email to their closest friends and family. Every other tactic is just icing on that email cake.

Don't acknowledge milestones, such as when an organizer hits their fundraising goal. If at all possible, in addition to any automated emails you may have set up, send a personal note or pick up the phone to give that organizer a sincere congratulations. Who knows, they may even increase their goal and keep the momentum going.

Don't customize, where possible, automated emails. As we've discussed elsewhere in this book, these automated robo-emails are actually a great opportunity to reinforce key messages and point to resources. There may be more personalization potential than you realize, so poke and play around.

Don't cross-promote on eNewsletters, websites, social, etc. While you may not integrate P2P opportunities into your year-end campaign, or an emergency appeal, it could very reasonably be integrated into your eNewsletters and social media calendars.

ADVOCACY APPEALS

Philanthropy and fundraising are rarely apolitical. We all see an inequity, a gap, an injustice or a need that isn't being met so we band together to fix it. Often, our work may just be a stop gap, because one or more levels of government might be far better suited to manage the programs and allocate the resources. Or, there is already a government program in place that is failing or mismanaged.

A definition of advocacy that we can build on is *when a charity is asking for public support with which to influence public policy and/or raise awareness on a specific issue.*

Advocacy appeals can be split into two distinct types:

1. **Formal**: engaging constituents to change or influence a public policy. Could be "Tell your MP to speak up by sending this letter today" or "Ask our Prime Minister to sign the UN Arms Trade Treaty."

2. **Informal/Lead Generation**: engaging individuals to publicly display their support for an issue and possibly take an action that is public. Could be "Sign our pledge to fight against cancer!" or "Pledge to show your support for Syrian refugees."

Formal advocacy is a subject deserving of its own book, not to mention the minefield of ethical and legal considerations you'll need to be mindful of along the way. Lead generation is far more often the domain of the fundraising team because it deepens loyalty, demonstrates accountability, and feeds your prospect pipelines in all sorts of ways by keeping your list growing. For the remainder of this book we'll focus only on the informal, or lead generation, type of advocacy.

The best advocacy (lead generation) campaigns:

Have a simple, powerful, urgent call to action. There's a balance to be struck here, and how you do it will be different each time. If the target of your campaign—the issue you're addressing—is too specific, it may not attract interest and engagement from outside your loyal base of supporters. If the ask is too nonspecific, it could be easily ignored and easily clocked as existing only to capture email addresses.

Clearly outline what you want supporters to do, and why. If you want them to sign a petition, make sure to communicate why you think a petition is the right tactic, and what you believe it will accomplish.

Are easily shareable by email and on social media. Deep down we all hope that our advocacy efforts will go viral, right? If you don't ensure that your appeal is easily shared on social media, you're not even giving it the tiny sliver of hope that *this may be the one*.

Can be understood at a glance. The headline and first sentence of your appeal is going to make that first impression with (hopefully) thousands of new supporters. Make it count, and remember the power of repetition and consistency to build momentum.

Track the source and behaviour of these new leads by ensuring they are added to your database, and that it's clear which advocacy action brought them in. You'll not only be able to report on the success of your campaign, you can also tailor future asks and actions to this now-known interest.

Have a strategy for converting pledgers to donors. If you have the tools and know-how, you might be able to automate a welcome and conversion series that kicks off after the initial signup. If you aren't yet able to automate this, you can still manually contact these supporters by isolating them in your database and grouping them as an audience in your email platform.

Common advocacy (lead generation) mistakes:

Launch, then go silent. With your fundraising appeals, the risk of going silent is that your revenue will dry up. The risk of going silent in an advocacy campaign is that you could appear to have cried wolf. If the need was so great, why only one email and a couple tweets?

Don't support the campaign with shareable content. By giving your community simple, professional-looking materials to share on social media, you can unlock access to hundreds, if not thousands, of new eyes and ears. Develop a wide array of shareables with a tool like Canva, and you'll have something for everyone.

Don't enlist influencers to increase reach. While I'm not a big champion of depending on celebrity support for fundraising, I do think that their influence can dramatically increase the reach of your appeal, and might also attract much-needed media attention.

Never seem to end, or at least report on progress. You know by now that your advocacy appeal shouldn't be a flash in the pan, but it certainly will have a shelf life. If your campaign carries on too long without some "wins" that you can celebrate, or updates on what might be happening behind the scenes, then you may be sending the message that you've given up or moved on from the issue.

ACTION COMES FROM KEEPING THE
HEAT ON. NO POLITICIAN CAN SIT
ON A HOT ISSUE IF YOU MAKE IT HOT
ENOUGH.

Saul Alinsky
Rules for Radicals

STEWARDSHIP EFFORTS

How you treat your charity's supporters after they've taken an action—whether a donation, or a non-financial action like a petition signature or volunteering—will have a direct impact on how much money you raise this year. This is because great stewardship improves retention rates, improves your average gift amount, and improves the results of your conversion efforts. Because of this, it is as important to strategize, plan and execute your stewardship efforts with the same enthusiasm and precision as your donation appeals.

Rather than labelling stewardship activities as an appeal, let's refer to them as "efforts." And, let's define these stewardship efforts as a *deliberate act of acknowledging support, regardless of whether in the form of philanthropy, volunteerism, or in-kind.* Stewardship efforts can be done in an intensive period of time, like a thank-a-thon, or they can just as reasonably be distributed over months or the course of a year, in which case you would want to refresh and revisit the activities on an annual basis.

Digital stewardship efforts come in near limitless forms. In my experience, a majority of them fit within one of these four categories:

1. **Thank Yous** that are automated or templated.
2. **Spotlights** on donors, volunteers.
3. **Impact Reporting** of past campaigns and programs

4. Organization Updates like Annual Reports.

The best stewardship efforts:

Are timely, which online likely means immediately after the donation (whereas offline you should aim for thanking no more than five business days after the gift). For large-scale efforts like a thank-a-thon, consider lining it up alongside a date that is meaningful to your charity, such as a national awareness day.

Are personalized. For your digital thank yous, you may want to set up alerts for gifts over a certain level, depending on what your charity considers a sizeable gift. This way you can send a direct, personal note to thank this person in addition to your automated email.

Are sincere. Stewardship touch points are not the time to regurgitate talking points and mission statements. This is when sincerity and authenticity need to shine.

Are donor-centric, meaning the emphasis throughout your efforts is about what the donor has made possible with their gift and how the donor drives this progress forward.

Common stewardship mistakes:

They don't happen at all. Sadly, this is still common and is often because stewardship has been prioritized very low on an incredibly long task list. We plan on getting around to it, but before we know it the next event or appeal is underway and the cycle repeats itself.

Are an afterthought to an appeal, which means if they happen at all, they are impersonal, poorly timed and poorly executed.

Happen so late, the donor forgot they gave. Yes, this also happens. Some shops may decide to batch together their receipts and acknowledgements for a handful of times in the year. Donors are likely supporting multiple charities, and if by the time your thank you rolls around they have forgotten they even gave, you've done your brand and the future of your fundraising program no favours.

CROWDFUNDING

There's a powerful allure toward crowdfunding in the charitable sector. Crowdfunding is when a project or venture is supported online by a large number of people, many of whom are giving in relatively small amounts.

Wait one second…that sounds familiar. You could say that for as long as charities have been asking for donations online (20+ years), we've actually just been crowdfunding. Crowdfunding campaigns typically involve:

1. A clearly **defined financial goal**.

2. A **specific program/project/product** if the goal is met.
3. **Small asks to many** people to hit the goal.
4. **Incentives** that increase in value with the value of the gift.

In the Venn diagram of traditional digital fundraising and crowdfunding, there is more overlap than there are distinct differences, and those differences are important to understand:

Often, if a crowdfunding goal isn't met, no money is transferred. People that support crowdfunding opportunities are enticed by the all or nothing agreement, possibly because they believe it to be a low/no risk proposition. Either they support a successful campaign, or their money never leaves the bank. In our line of work, we will accept and put to use all donations as they are received, even if we fall short of a target we may have set for ourselves.

Crowdfunding can incentivize without concern for legal frameworks and regulation. Canadian charities have limitations on the value of gift recognition (if the fair market value of the gift exceeds 10% of the donation amount or $75, the value needs to be deducted from the gift receipt). If you are outside Canada, you should brush up on what laws apply. For a crowdfunding campaign, it's not uncommon to see incentives like a T-shirt for a $50 donation, which unquestionably exceeds the 10% rule. Charities can still provide incentives, but you'll need to be more creative than T-shirts, DVDs or concert tickets. Consider things like facility tours, coffee with the founder, or naming something in their honour.

The best ones are GREAT at cheering on support, and providing updates. This is one area where charities are getting our butts kicked by crowdfunding startups. Creators are constantly creating and sharing video updates, thanking supporters, and adding new incentives to keep interest high.

A recent innovation in crowdfunding worth noting is the rise in monthly subscription platforms like Patreon that allow people to give a monthly "gift" to directly support a creator. Artists and creators that fill a *very* specific niche are best suited to these platforms, particularly video game streamers, cosplayers, podcast producers, and investigative journalists.

A last word of caution about crowdfunding: it's important to keep in mind that *anyone* can set up a crowdfunding campaign for *anything*. Crowdfunding was largely born out of necessity for artists and entrepreneurs that were not able to access traditional forms of capital to make their ideas a reality. Charities have access to a variety of funding sources that a for-profit corporation does not—public and private foundation grants, for example— along with the ability to issue official donation receipts that can be used to reduce personal income tax.

FOR MOST PROJECTS, KICKSTARTER ISN'T THE ANSWER TO THE QUESTION YOU'RE ASKING. THAT'S BECAUSE IT COULD MORE ACCURATELY BE CALLED *KICKFINISHER*—YOU BUILD A FOLLOWING FIRST, OVER TIME, AND THEN KICKSTARTER IS THE MOMENT IN TIME THAT THOSE FOLLOWERS SHOW UP FOR YOUR WORK.

Seth Godin

2.
SOCIAL MEDIA

L et's get a basic definition of social media out of the way! Social media boils down to *websites and applications that enable users to create and share content or to participate in social networking*. The key words there are *create* and *share*, which is where the true divergence from the pre-social media internet can be pinpointed. Prior to social media, websites were made and they were consumed. Interaction between internet users was limited to the vibrant yet small pockets of activity on bulletin boards, forums, message boards, and Geocities pages.

Whether we are active participants in social media or not, our lives are very much steeped in influence and power that is wielded via social media. Headline news is broken on social media, current and future political leaders use it to stoke fears and division, and online retailers have shopping malls on life support. It's also where billions of friends and family members stay connected, send birthday greetings and condolences. It's where artists and creators have found new audiences, and where survivors have been empowered to speak truth to power about police brutality, racism, sexual assault, and much more.

Because of all this, I've wavered over the past decade in my opinion about how valuable social media is in a digital fundraising program, and whether we have over- or under-valued it. What always brings me back to the pro-social media side of the argument is the potential it has to bring about rapid social change by powering social movements with tools that are far more accessible and democratically distributed than anything our predecessors had at their disposal.

In their study, *Reframing Issues in the Digital Age: Using Social Media Strategically,* Julie Sweetland, PhD, and Rob Shore clocked that, as the world of mass communications moves away from a broadcast model of information sharing to a networked, social engagement model, the tools of opinion-making are now in the hands of advocates. But the medium is not the message, and the tools, if not used with care, can have little—or even harmful—effect.

In this chapter we'll cover the fundamentals, but then pivot to the ways in which you can maximize the potential benevolent impact that social media has to advance your mission.

In no particular order, charities tend most often to use social media for one of six activities:

1. Advertising & Promotion
2. Community Building
3. Fundraising
4. Advocacy
5. Organizing (including special events)
6. Relationship Building

Whatever uses you have for social media, and whatever strategies you choose to employ, there is one undeniable thread that runs through all great social media programs: **value**. At every stage, ask yourself if what you're sharing will be perceived by your supporters as having value. Value on social media often means helping supporters feel happier, more aware, useful, engaged, or better educated.

BENEFITS OF SOCIAL MEDIA

Immediate benefits of social media for charities include:

Account ownership is free, and takes minutes. You'll need to pay in order to promote your brand, and getting your profile design *just right* will take more than a few minutes. Once you're up and running, invite your current supporters, staff and volunteers to come follow you on the platform. Getting a small boost in your follower numbers will help attract others, and will ensure your first posts won't go ignored.

Basic functions are familiar and easy to use. As your following grows, you'll be able to poll, share video, host live discussions and panels, and so much more. These are not just great ways to show your followers that you're engaged, it also gives you plenty of new data and analytics behind the scenes that will help you strategize and optimize future campaigns.

A bunch of your supporters may already be there. On the big five platforms (which we'll look at shortly), you may already have fans that are ready and willing to interact with you there. This will help you expand awareness of your brand and programming.

The longer-term benefits of social media for charities are:

Recruit support (likes, donations) from friends of friends. When trying to attract new supporters, your best results will come from the people that are closest to your existing circle of friends. For your organic posts, encourage your followers to share or retweet your content. For paid advertisements, creating lookalike audiences (see the definitions at the end of this chapter for more detail on this) will give you a much better ROI.

Target audiences by demographics, geography, behaviour. As your confidence and skill set as a page administrator grows, you'll be able to get more savvy with how you strategize and spend a social media budget to attract new supporters who have no existing connection to your cause. The more personalized and segmented you can make your promotions, the better.

Deepen the understanding of your audience. As your following grows, you'll have access to various reports that will tell you quite a bit about your audience—genders, age distribution, locations, or shopping habits. This sort of data is incredibly important to potential corporate sponsors, as well as to some grantors that want to be sure there is alignment between your audience and theirs.

POPULAR PLATFORMS

There are dozens of social media platforms that are available to charities, but at the time of writing this in 2020 there are 5 that I think charities should **strongly consider** using to build their online following.

1. **Facebook**. As the global leader in active monthly users, it is very likely that a majority of your supporters have an account, and a large number of those are still active. The active users will skew older (57% of users are over 35), which is in fact good news if you're leveraging the platform for fundraising. Depending on your country, there are varying tools built into the platform for fundraising,

but given rising concerns about privacy and data protection, it would be wise to engage and interact on the platform but complete the donations off-platform on your website.

2. **YouTube**. This stalwart of video sharing can be home base for any video content you may create, not to mention the growing suite of tools that they offer for editing video. Take the time to ensure your channel page is up to date and on-brand, and that each of your videos have a descriptive title, description and associated keywords. All of this helps people find your videos. You can also host a live broadcast which, while not a new feature of YouTube, is finding new value in times of physical distancing. It's worth noting that YouTube is owned by Google.

3. **Instagram**. While it started as a photo sharing app, the addition of Stories and IGTV have made it possible to get creative with more long-form video. This platform prioritizes the mobile experience, meaning that while you can visit Instagram in a desktop browser, that is not—and likely never will be—the intended experience. It's worth noting that Instagram is currently owned by Facebook.

4. **LinkedIn**. This business- and career-focused platform skews toward an older user, and some evidence suggests that the average level of education completed is higher than on other large social networks. The conversation and content here centres around business, networking, self-promotion

and hiring. Charities would be wise to create and maintain a company page, and encourage staff and board members who are LinkedIn users to ensure the career section of their personal pages links to the organization's official page.

5. **Twitter**. This now ubiquitous "micro-blogging" platform would be easy to dismiss, if it weren't for the fact that it is still so influential as a source for breaking news, spotting trending topics, and real-time commentary on current events. For your charity's page, I recommend quality over quantity. When you tweet about your current campaign or appeal, pin it to the top of your timeline. Follow accounts that are active in your sector, and respond to DMs and @ mentions as soon as you're able.

There are four other platforms that I think you should **consider and explore** to see if they are right for your charity:

1. **TikTok**. This app lets users create quick, snappy videos and choose from tons of trendy filters and effects, as well as ways to mash up their video alongside those of other users. A main feature of the app is the 'For You' page (FYP for short), where TikTok will show you videos from other users that you may or may not already follow. It doesn't take long for the app to get a sense of what your interests are based on how you react to its suggestions, and the result is a FYP that can be

eerily accurate. What this might mean for your charity is that if you create content that is true to your brand voice, the algorithm will do the audience targeting for you.

2. **Reddit**. While the user interface is not the most modern, Reddit does have a large, loyal and active user base. If you aren't among them, Reddit in a nutshell is a site for users to post a link to a news article, image, or even just pose a question to the community. While Reddit refers to the website and community as a whole, it is in fact a collection of smaller sub-communities called subreddits. Users can vote the post up or down, which theoretically brings the most popular content to the top of the subreddit, and the hottest posts make their way to the front page of Reddit. For valid and well-documented reasons, the Reddit community has a reputation for being quite toxic. However in recent years the company (owned by media giant Condé Nast) has been more actively scrubbing the site of hateful and problematic subreddits.

3. **Twitch**. This platform is primarily for live-streaming video game play with real-time commentary from the person at the controls. If you're not a gamer, you may not realize how quickly the video game industry has grown in recent years. It's larger than the music and film industry *combined*. The entry point for charities into this world is less obvious than for Facebook or Instagram, but there remains a tremendous

opportunity for an increasing number of charities to engage with the gaming community and tap into the massive amount of money being spent.

4. **Snapchat**. If you haven't used it, Snapchat is essentially a messaging platform that allows you to send a photo or video to one or many people, and the message disappears after it's been viewed. It is possible to screen capture a photo, but the creator of the video will know that you've done so. It's most often associated with being an app for sexting—and it certainly is that—but that is not its intended use. Younger users appreciate the ephemeral nature of the platform, often feeling like they can be more honest and open in the app with friends, as opposed to an Instagram or Facebook that will be public for years to come.

Not discussed above, but I feel a responsibility to mention, are popular instant messaging apps like WhatsApp, Facebook Messenger, and QQ which have massive user bases. These are less feature-rich than Instagram or Snapchat, but there are billions of chats and group messages happening on them, and users from every corner of the world. There are also several social media platforms like WeChat, QZone, Sina Weibo and Kuaishou that have millions (or in WeChat's case, over a billion) active monthly users. They are primarily used in China or by Mandarin speakers outside China. Recently, Chinese Canadians—nearly a month ahead of provincially-mandated COVID-19 lockdowns—were self-organizing on WeChat to deliver groceries and goods to people that were self-quarantining after having either travelled to Hubei province, or coming in contact with someone who had.

A note at this point about privacy and data security feels necessary. While social media use continues to grow, there is a groundswell of conversation and concern about what data mining may be happening, what surveillance might be happening, and what effects it might be having on our physical and mental health. These conversations are relevant to charities and fundraising insofar as there is reputational risk when your brand is on any of these platforms. If you're a mental health charity, you should be considering how you may be contributing to social media addiction. If you're a human rights charity, you may want to have prepared statements on your justification for using a platform that might be silencing or monitoring the behaviour of certain users. An environmental charity might want to consider the environmental impact of the massive data centres that power the cloud computing capabilities of these tools.

RETURN ON INVESTMENT

The most frustrating and elusive factor in a social media strategy or program is calculating return on investment (ROI). This is because inside a single platform like Facebook or Twitter, it isn't too hard to see. These platforms have their own analytics dashboards that generate great reports. Taking that data out of the social media platform, then linking it to a separate list—such as a list of donations—can be difficult, time-consuming, or simply not possible under certain conditions. Your best chance at tracking specific revenue from social media is to use eCommerce tracking, which with some work, can do detailed attribution with the use of cookies that track behaviours.

Common ways to calculate ROI on social:

Using conversion pixels in your website and donation forms. Facebook, Instagram, and Twitter each have a snippet of code that can be added to your donation form which will unlock the ability to see exactly how much revenue can be attributed to each advertisement. This type of measurement and reporting only applies to paid social media advertising, not to organic/unpaid posts.

eCommerce tracking in Google Analytics, combined with link building. We discussed each of these in more detail in our Analytics chapter. The benefit of this measurement strategy is that it allows you to better understand how your organic posts perform. In this scenario, the administrative reports within the social media platform won't tell you the exact revenue you've generated, but a Google Analytics report will be able to detail the conversion value of each unique link.

Creating custom donation forms, so gifts can be easily identified. This is a less technologically-sophisticated and more time-intensive strategy, but it's far better than having no data at all. If the tool or platform you are using for your web donation forms makes it easy to duplicate an existing form, then take advantage of this feature and link to these forms when you post a donation ask on social media. From the visitor's perspective it may look no different than any other form associated with your campaign, but from within your online donation system you should be able to generate reports for each of these custom forms.

SOCIAL MEDIA GUIDELINES

A social media policy is a *corporate code of conduct that provides guidelines for employees who post content on the Internet either as part of their job or as a private person.* It's wise to make one while setting up your profiles, or if you already have profiles but no policy, now is the time to create your first.

Why have one? To protect your brand, staff, and volunteers.

Who writes them? Management with departmental input.

Who approves them? Board of directors

Who enforces them? Management with board oversight.

A good social media policy or guideline is revisited regularly to ensure it evolves to meet the ever-changing online environment and organizational needs. There are *plenty* of free templates online that are just a Google search away.

ENGAGEMENT STRATEGIES

Charities have an incredible competitive advantage over their for-profit counterparts. Our 'product' enriches their lives, as well as others', in a way that few tangible products can, certainly more than a new pair of shoes, or a hotel room. For-profit companies' competitive advantage over charities online are their budgets, and their expertise on how to spend those budgets. The best digital fundraisers strategize and spend with shrewd business acumen, but also tell great stories and tap into a reservoir of emotion that only we can.

Engage authentically. Respond to questions quickly, ask questions, and if you're dealing with a troll you can opt to respond, hide their post, comment, or delete their posts altogether.

Do not automate duplicate content between social networks. Your channels can share themes and messages. They should not share the posts themselves. You lose the ability to optimize for length, timing, and the ideal image dimensions. For example, do not use a service that automatically posts an update to Twitter when you update your Facebook status, or use a service that automatically shares an image to Facebook when you post to Instagram.

Be a content curator. Don't be shy about sharing content made by others that will be of interest to your audience. Tips: Consider the source and share from trusted sources only. If it's not clear (such as a direct link), credit and tag the source. Layer on your opinion/context, justifying why you've shared.

Tap into breaking news and current affairs to show that your charity is tuned in. Your cause can also provide valuable context and commentary to the news of the day, which only strengthens your reputation as a thought leader.

Use strong visuals in your social media posts, enabling you to reach more of your audience, and have higher rates of engagement. Visuals inspire higher interaction and engagement rates. On Facebook, you'll reach more users organically and your followers will be more likely to like, comment and share, thus extending your unpaid reach. On Twitter, you'll be more likely to get retweeted, thus attracting new followers and advocates. Some golden rules of social images:

⋯→ **Keep the number of subjects low**. 1-3 people, animals, or trees.

⋯→ **If using pictures of people, eye contact is ideal**. If not, 'action' shots are great, e.g. showing movement and emotion.

⋯→ **If sharing stats, keep them simple.** One stat per image. Ask yourself how easily someone would be able to recall the statistic in conversation.

STORYTELLING

If you want to separate yourself from the pack, and build a loyal audience, you need to **prioritize storytelling over marketing**. We are all inundated with advertising, often watered down to generic tag lines and sales tactics. Our charitable brands have a deep well of compelling stories to draw from—far more than a company selling soap or sugar water.

'Storytelling' has been a buzzword for years now in fundraising. I'm certain that by now, fundraisers understand *why* storytelling is important, but I'm not convinced that a majority of us know *how* to tell great stories. Good news! Storytelling is not a mysterious, innate skill that only a select few fundraisers are born with. It can be learned, and doesn't have to be a black box any longer.

There is a pattern of storytelling that you're no doubt familiar with, even if you haven't yet had the vocabulary to describe it. The academic Joseph Campbell coined the term "the hero's journey" in 1949 and it's stuck. This is no doubt because the familiar structure resonates emotionally, improves recall, and more often than not provides a satisfactory or compelling resolution.

<u>The component parts of the hero's journey</u>:

1. A character is in a zone of comfort,
2. But they want something.
3. They enter an unfamiliar situation,
4. Adapt to it,
5. Get what they wanted,
6. Pay a heavy price for it,
7. Then return to their familiar situation,
8. Having changed.

Don't be fooled into thinking that this format only applies to writing novels, screenplays or long-form appeals. It's a structure that you can strive for in a format as brief as a 280-character tweet. The hero's journey is also a helpful tool as you listen to the stories of people that have benefitted from your charity and its programs. If you're feeling stuck when writing your story, refer back to this structure and find the spot where your protagonist is situated, and you'll get a sense of where to go next. Not every one of the eight steps is going to suit your storytelling needs, but it will send you in the right direction and help you snap your story back to a familiar narrative structure.

If you're not convinced that this structure is necessary, or as pervasive as I'm trying to convince you it is, then think of the most popular films of the last few decades: Star Wars, Shrek, Harry Potter, Spiderman, Lord of the Rings. They are all deliberately structured around one or more hero's journey stories. We also see it in popular music—a simple chord progression evolves into an ear worm chorus, descends into a dark bridge, followed by a return to the catchy chorus that gives listeners a feeling of familiarity and comfort.

If you're in the position of writing copy for your appeals, here is one example of how you might structure a beneficiary story using the story circle:

1. Hafsa remembers a peaceful childhood in Uganda.
2. She was attending school, dreaming of being a doctor.
3. Rebel groups killed her parents, but she escaped.
4. In a Kenyan refugee camp, *Charity A* was able to help.
5. With the help of a scholarship, Hafsa is attending school.
6. She couldn't save her parents' lives, or bring them back.
7. But she plans to return to her village, and to rebuild.
8. Bright minds like Hafsa are Uganda's future.

What we see in this story circle example is how we can structure how we tell the story of our charity's beneficiaries. Simultaneously, you'll need to weave your donor into the story as well, because with an understanding of how and where they fit into the story, the better they'll be able to understand how they can help. Here's what that might look like:

1. Hafsa remembers a peaceful childhood in Uganda
   A. *Your childhood memories are precious, and important.*

2. She was attending school, dreaming of being a doctor.
   B. *What did you want to be when you grew up?*

3. Rebel groups killed her parents, but she escaped.
   C. *Life gets busy, and complicated though, doesn't it?*

4. In a Kenyan refugee camp, *Charity A* was able to help.
   D. *When times got tough, did you have a guardian angel?*

5. With the help of a scholarship, Hafsa is attending school.
   E. *Did the kindness and love of others get you through?*

6. She couldn't save her parents' lives, or bring them back.
   F. *The struggles made you who you are, didn't they?*

7. But she plans to return to her village, and to rebuild.
   G. *You may have grown up, but that child is still inside.*

8. Bright minds like Hafsa are Uganda's future.
   H. *While children dream, adults can take action.*

The above may sound formulaic, because it is. But to your donors, it is far more likely to feel familiar. In fundraising, familiar is your friend, because when you tap into your donor's habits and routines, you have far less heavy lifting to do. If you are adamant that you need to shake up the formula, my suggestion is to consider starting your story *in media res,* or "in the middle of things" which is a common tactic for filmmakers. Take *Star Wars: A New Hope* for example. It is a quintessential story circle structure—George Lucas has specifically said so—yet, the film begins in the throes of a battle sequence.

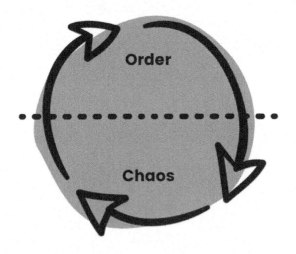

Source: Channel 101 wiki, available:
channel101.fandom.com

The hero's journey is an imperfect starting point, but it's a starting point nonetheless. Kurt Vonnegut went through a similar exercise of mapping story structures, because, as he put it, "[…]stories have shapes which can be drawn on graph paper, and the shape of a given society's stories is at least as interesting as the shape of its pots or spearheads." Vonnegut sketched out eight structures:

1. Man in Hole
2. Boy Meets Girl
3. From Bad to Worse
4. Which Way is Up?
5. Creation Story
6. Old Testament
7. New Testament
8. Cinderella

Vonnegut believed every story could be charted along an x-axis that represented time, and a y-axis that represented the rise and fall of good things happening to the protagonist. Again, these are imperfect starting points, but starting points nonetheless. They are also all imperfect because, being written by men, there is explicit and implicit masculine bias throughout. The authors are also white, so there are flaws of implicit bias that omit facts and realities of structural racism throughout our society. These flaws can't be overlooked, but I do hope that by acknowledging them outright we can build newer, more equitable frameworks for telling great stories.

COMMON SOCIAL MEDIA TERMS

So that you have them handy, here are some basic definitions of terms you're likely to hear as you journey deeper into the world of social media administration.

Organic Reach: The total number of unique people who were shown your post through unpaid distribution.

Paid Reach: The total number of unique people who were shown your post as a result of ads.

Social Media Dashboard: A social media management tool that individuals or companies can use to coordinate a social media presence across multiple channels or accounts, through a single interface.

Inbound Marketing: Focuses on earning, not buying, a person's attention, which is done through social media and engaging content, such as blogs, podcasts and white papers. This content is interesting, informative and adds value, creating a positive connection. Inbound (or, content) marketing relies on desirable content being shared on social media (Facebook, Twitter) and aggregator sites (Reddit, Feedly, Flipbook) for these strategies to work. Opposite of "Outbound Marketing" which is the more traditional approach of sending messages outward, which could be direct mail, TV ads, or email. It is also known as "content marketing", "earned media" or "marketing you don't hate."

Social Media Automation: The use of an online tool to schedule the release of content at a future time and date, and in some cases, automate routine tasks and workflows. Examples: scheduling a post to launch on Saturday morning, so you don't have to work on the weekend. In Facebook, you can write an auto-response for messages like *"Hi [name], we'll look into that and get back to you soon. Cheers!"*

Audiences: Paid social media marketing allows advertisers like you an incredible amount of control over which audiences they are speaking to. This can be done by identifying and isolating audiences using combinations of tools:

⇢ **Audience insights** give you the ability to select an audience based on what the search engine or social media platform can tell are the user's interests and online buying habits.

⇢ **Custom audience matching** is the ability to upload an email list that you have permission to use, and if those same emails were used to create the users' social media accounts, then you'll be able to target them specifically for your advertisements.

⇢ **Lookalike audiences** are created by using one *known* audience (a common one is people who like your Facebook page) to create a new audience that shares similar interests, location, age, and any other data points that their targeting can draw in. This is often an effective way of finding like-minded people who don't yet know about your work.

Social Media Engagement: When used broadly, this is simply the interaction between people and brands on social networks. On each given social media or advertising platform, "engagement" can in fact mean something very specific. On Facebook, Engagement Rate is a metric that represents the number of comments, shares, clicks, and likes as a percentage of the total people a post reached.

3.
DIGITAL JOURNEYS

F ar too often, if not always, charities are at the receiving end of a breakup. It's rarely a nasty breakup though—more of a "we drifted apart" type of unraveling, if not being altogether ghosted.

We're a needy bunch, us fundraisers. We have lofty visions of acquiring young donors that will stick by us from the schoolyard to the graveyard, only to find out they've met someone new—and just as they've started to earn a disposable income, no less. It's not as though fundraisers haven't been sounding the alarm to this issue for decades now. Ken Burnett's landmark text **Relationship Fundraising** was first published in 1992 on a simple premise:

> *[Relationship fundraising is] an approach to the marketing of a cause which centres not around*

raising money but on developing to its full potential the unique and special relationship that exists between a charity and its supporter. Whatever strategies and techniques are employed to boost funds, the overriding consideration in relationship fundraising is to care for and develop that special bond.

David Dunlop and G.T. "Buck" Smith at Cornell University formalized the process of **moves management**, which is a *set of processes nonprofits rely on to develop constituent relationships and move them toward major giving*. A well-executed moves management protocol enables you to focus on developing donors—rather than simply securing donations.

From these sturdy foundations—relationship fundraising and moves management—a hybrid has emerged in recent years that is versatile and effective for digital fundraising purposes: **the donor journey.** When viewed as a whole, a donor's journey from start to finish is a term we give to the sum and sequence of interactions that each supporter has with a charity. Our task as savvy digital fundraisers is to support and shape this journey, while also responding to new data and insights as they emerge, so that we can pivot and optimize along the way.

In Section II we took a deep dive into design thinking, and that mindset will serve you well when planning and managing donor journeys. Rather than viewing donor journeys as a linear path from A to Z, you'll manage much better by viewing journeys as a series of loops and cycles that ultimately edge and trend toward their inevitable end—death, of course. A tool has been developed to help us do just this, to plan to the best of our ability a donor's journey. It's called donor journey mapping, and what's most important is that you put pen to paper to make your version 1.0 of a donor journey. Because, without that version 1.0, there can never be a version 1.1, 1.2, 2.0, 3.0 and so on. Here are some words of wisdom from practitioners that have seen the power of donor journey mapping firsthand:

The primary purpose of [the donor lifecycle map] is to show the correlation of donor value with engagement, both of which, of course, should be growing!

Sarah Clifton
Head of Fundraising, Save the Children
Netherlands

A fabulous piece of thinking, as it helps charities to see all of their programmes mapped out; how each programme can draw prospects from other programmes, offering donors new propositions, products and gift levels.

Tony Elischer
Founder, THINK Consulting Solutions Inc.

We are so focused on the current campaign, whether it is annual or capital or both, that we don't pay attention to the macro-view to the number of discrete donative possibilities that we provide to an individual over time.

Deborah Kaplan Polivy
Donor Cultivation and the Donor Lifecycle Map

Digital fundraising and engagement with supporters has added complexity and nuance to relationship management, with no chance of slowing down. The sooner you can begin mapping out your Donor Journey 1.0, the better. So, **where does a journey start**? This is a deceptively simple question. Is it the first time they hear about your charity? At the first action they take, which could be an email signup, or Facebook like? When the donor gives their first gift? It depends. It depends on the brand awareness the charity has, on the capacity that its staff has, and on the charity's marketing mix (or lack of marketing at all).

An advocacy organization's journey may begin when the first petition is signed. A hospital foundation's may start when you walk in the emergency room doors in need of care. A university foundation donor's journey may start before they've left high school, when their acceptance letter arrives in the mail.

As you sketch out a journey, you'll need to ask: **when does a donor's journey end**? When the donor hasn't given for 2, 5, or 10 years? When the donor requests no further contact? When the donor dies?

Again, it depends. Ideally, a donor "loves us to death" by giving a gift in their Will. Others may want to give a major gift while they are alive. Donors may leave, or cease giving to a charity because of personal reasons, through no fault of the charity. Donors may leave because they don't feel their needs or expectations are being met. And often, it ends because of a situation that the charity often has no control over, such as a major health issue or job loss.

As you map this out—I've included some basic workflow examples that may help you get started—it's important that your version 1.0 can be realistically achieved and maintained. Here are a few questions to ask yourself, or your team if you're doing this together, that will help ground your plan in a practical reality:

1. Do we have the **tools** to do what we are proposing?
2. Do we have the technical **expertise** to build this?
3. What do we expect will happen at each stage, why, and how will we know if that happens?
4. What can be **automated**, and what can not?
5. Do we have, or can we justify, the **time** to do this?
6. If it breaks, can we **fix** it ourselves?

All of the above of course is in addition to the tried and true practices for project management—assigning the appropriate and right-sized team, setting out a clear timeline and milestones, establishing clear approval stages and a thorough plan for testing before it's live.

What I have not done for you in this chapter is provide a simple, turnkey journey that you can copy and paste for your charity. If that's frustrating—I get it. I highly recommend that you reach out to a few of your digital fundraising peers and ask to see what (if anything) they have documented for their donor journeys. Ask them what is working, what isn't, what they wish they'd done differently, and what they plan on trying but haven't gotten around to yet. You'll learn far more from having three of these conversations than any single solution I could provide you with here. I have given you a very basic grid template that can get you started, but it's only meant to get you started with the process. Swipe it, mess with it, and make it yours. Project it onto a whiteboard, order a pizza, invite some teammates and go to town on filling in the blanks of what an ideal journey for a current or future donor might look like.

Filmmaker and YouTube vlogging pioneer Casey Neistat lives by a motto of "customize everything" which influences everything from his movies, his personal style, and the design aesthetic of his clothes and production studio. Customizing everything also serves some very specific, functional needs to optimize your time and efforts. While sketching out your donor journeys, you have to consider function and efficiency along the way. The strongest first swing at your donor journey mapping will be the plan that strikes a balance between the limitations of your tools and time, and giving donors and supporters a memorable and meaningful set of interactions with your charity.

DONOR LOYALTY

This is why we do it. Everything in this book, for this. The key to an effective donor journey in one word: loyalty.

Without an overwhelming emphasis on donor loyalty and retention, there is no donor journey, because there is no second gift. Rigorous academic research, particularly by Dr. Adrian Sargeant, Dr. Jen Shang, and Elaine Jay has deepened our profession's understanding of donor loyalty, and in the process uncovered significant gaps in status quo fundraising practice. I highly recommend you seek out and read Dr. Sargeant's 2008 paper *"Donor Retention: What Do We Know and What Can We Do About It?"* which holds up incredibly well over a decade later. In it, he lays out four key factors in donor loyalty and retention that you would be well served to commit to memory:

Satisfaction: A donor's evaluation of service quality.
Identification: Satisfying the need for a social identity.
Commitment: Building or establishing 'stickiness'.
Trust: Believing one's needs will be fulfilled.

Over the past decade, these principles have been proven true with quantitative analysis, as well as qualitatively in case studies throughout Canada, the US and UK. If you've been to a fundraising conference lately and been blown away by a great case study, there's a good chance that in order to achieve that impressive number of new donors and the amazing ROI, there was also a sound execution of basics that contributed to satisfaction, identification, commitment, and trust.

Every fundraiser, digital-focused or otherwise, needs to have these four factors committed to memory. They may be slightly more ambiguous than technical aspects of your program, like unsubscribe rates or search rankings, but they are no less important.

In the earlier chapter *Thinking in Systems*, we acknowledged that the tolerance of ambiguity is a sign of maturity, and an essential skill of a systems-thinking fundraiser. Pursuing, measuring, and optimizing for donor loyalty is where systems thinkers really thrive, because while there are some effective, established practices for strengthening loyalty, there is near-limitless space for creativity and personalization.

The building of loyalty starts well before the first gift. It can look like:

⇢ Responding quickly to inquiries through email, social media or phone regardless of a donor's giving history.

⇢ Demonstrating leadership on a topic in the media, and at events.

In my experience, far too many charities forget that the soft skills we employ with donors as part of a relationship fundraising approach can, and should, be incorporated before a donor's first gift. Often, a more impersonal and aggressive mindset is employed before a conversion. You see it in the language we hear, with terms like: market opportunities, audience identification, lead acquisition, activation, and cart abandonments. After a donor gives their first gift is when we start to hear more donor-centric language enter our analysis and strategies. We hear softer terms, like stewardship, communications, engagement, touch points.

I believe there's room for balance and compromise. It is possible to make data-driven decisions to maximize return, while questioning if we are starting a donor's journey in a thoughtful, empathetic and respectful manner. We should never lose touch with the fact that how we acquire new donors sets the tone for how they interpret each communication and interaction that follows.

OVER 70% OF PEOPLE THAT WE RECRUIT NEVER MAKE ANOTHER GIFT.

Dr. Adrian Sargeant
Co-Director
Institute for Sustainable Philanthropy

Journey Map

AUDIENCE:
_____

E.g., New Donors, Petition Signers,
Lapsed Donors, etc.

OBJECTIVE
_____
What are you aspiring to
achieve expressed as words

GOAL(s)
_____
What SMART goals will serve as
stepping stones along the way

STRATEGY
_____
Key insights informing how
and where you focus

MEASURE(s)
_____
Specific objective behaviours
and activities to measure

Touch #1	Touch #2	Touch #3	Touch #4

SECTION IV:
BURN IT DOWN

At some point six or seven years ago, I lost interest in books about fundraising, blogs about fundraising, podcasts about fundraising, presentations about fundraising, and so on. I felt some guilt about this because I know how hard my peers work to gather and share their knowledge. I wondered if it was a sign that maybe I should step away and pursue a whole new profession. I still enjoyed my work though, especially interacting with donors. I also still felt like there was so much ground for our profession to cover. So, I struck a balance by staying focused at work, while outside the office I began tugging at some threads that had been within reach for decades but never pulled. I cleared out my iTunes queue, and restocked it with new podcasts about design, architecture, science fiction, philosophy, and pop culture. Before long, I was having far more ideas and inspiration for fundraising than I ever did reading or listening to fundraising content.

This habit of finding inspiration in unconventional spaces and bringing it back to the fundraising sector was a turning point for me. The projects that spun out from these ideas—whether they were successful or not—helped me to gain some credibility as being a creative, innovative fundraiser. I am feeling most fulfilled when I am bridging traditional tactics and strategies with interesting and novel applications. Whether you've picked up this book because you're new to the profession, or you're a veteran who wants to bring your digital program up to snuff, I highly encourage you stay curious in the areas of your life that are far from being related to fundraising.

One source of inspiration came from the late 1960's in the form of a DIY book called the Whole Earth Catalog. Nowadays the Whole Earth Catalog might be best known for the four-word farewell on the back cover of their last edition, "stay hungry, stay foolish" which Steve Jobs quoted in a viral commencement speech at Stanford in 2005.

Stewart Brand and a collective of collaborators, published the first Whole Earth Catalog out of an earnest pursuit to understand and explore the many systems we all live in, how they interlock, and how we

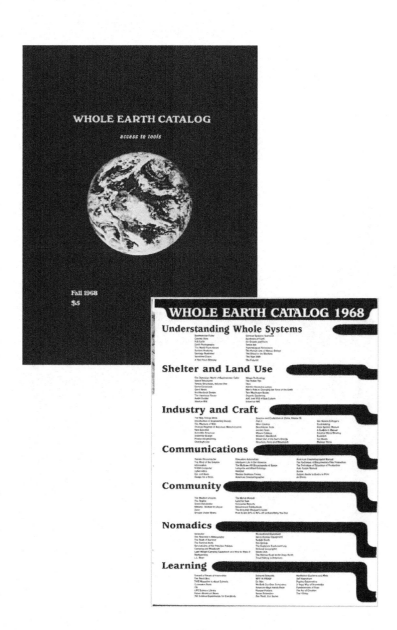

Excerpts from Whole Earth Catalog (Fall 1968) accessible via:
https://archive.org/details/1stWEC-complete/

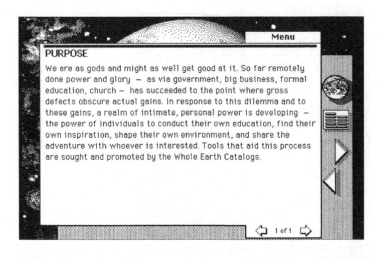

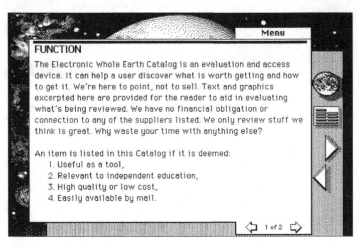

Screenshots from The Electronic Whole Earth Catalog (1988):
https://archive.org/details/the-electronic-whole-earth-catalog.

as humans might best integrate and move through them in a responsible way. Brand summed up the catalog's purpose with just three words on the front cover: **access to tools**. It was very much a catalog, in that it was a curated list of guides, magazines, novels, and manuals that were accompanied by a short description and instructions on how to purchase it directly from the author or publisher. What made the catalog so fascinating was the ethos they were able to articulate in the marginalia, imagery, and the curation itself—the juxtaposition of geodesic dome blueprints and an introduction to beekeeping just pages away from computer building guides (in 1968!), cybernetics and a text on the mind of a dolphin sent a clear message that life within a "whole system" is both rife with contradiction and ambiguity, but also a heck of a lot of fun.

Another well of inspiration is the work of architect and design thinker, Christopher Alexander. His most lauded work, "A Pattern Language" was released in 1977. In it, he describes 253 distinct "patterns" which are features within our built environments that solve a specific problem. For example, a doorway is a pattern, in that it is the solution to the common problem of needing to separate one room's purpose from another. But there are hundreds, if not thousands of variations on how to design a door. The patterns nest within each other, from the largest pattern, "town" right down to the smallest, "things from your life." As patterns are put to use and they interlock, they begin to form a language—not so dissimilar from the ways that we connect words to form sentences within a language. What set Alexander's text apart from earlier architectural writing was that it blurred the lines between practical functionality and philosophical treatise on how we might create metaphysical spaces for creativity, empathy and connection within the physical spaces that protect us from the elements. Throughout this book and each time I'm fortunate enough to present or lecture, I try to subtly do the same. Fulfill a practical need, but signal an awareness that there is a network of possibilities and applications just below the surface.

The idea that we live and work within languages fascinates me to no end. The bulk of this book can be read as a series of patterns that interlock to describe your digital fundraising programs and strategies. But if this is true, it's more dictionary than novel. It's what you'll refer to as you craft your own story, and others craft theirs, and we all contribute to a larger, growing body of knowledge. Alexander and his co-authors tout their method as "a timeless way of building," because while they proposed a general approach for solving problems, they weren't explicit in exactly how to build it. They left that up to us. I've thought a lot about "A Pattern Language" while writing this book, and have tried to provide you with general approaches, and leaving the specific design execution to you.

This leads into my last diversion, which comes from the world of visual arts. In a 2015 interview with author Steven Johnson, Brian Eno cracked open a whole new space in my brain with this statement:

A Pattern Language

Towns · Buildings · Construction

Christopher Alexander
Sara Ishikawa · Murray Silverstein
<small>WITH</small>
Max Jacobson · Ingrid Fiksdahl-King
Shlomo Angel

All 253 patterns together form a language. They create a coherent picture of an entire region, with the power to generate such regions in a million forms, with infinite variety in all the details.

It is also true that any small sequence of patterns from this language is itself a language for a smaller part of the environment; and this small list of patterns is then capable of generating a million parks, paths, houses, workshops, or gardens.

For example, consider the following ten patterns:

PRIVATE TERRACE ON THE STREET (140)
SUNNY PLACE (161)
OUTDOOR ROOM (163)
SIX-FOOT BALCONY (167)
PATHS AND GOALS (120)
CEILING HEIGHT VARIETY (190)
COLUMNS AT THE CORNERS (212)
FRONT DOOR BENCH (242)
RAISED FLOWERS (245)
DIFFERENT CHAIRS (251)

This short list of patterns is itself a language: it is one of a thousand possible languages for a porch, at the front of a house. One of us chose this small language, to build

There is a hangover of romantic assumptions of art, that art intrinsically has "something." I don't think art intrinsically has very much at all. I think that nearly everything that it has is conferred upon it by our collective history of experiencing art. So, we create the value. I think when something is exciting to you—a picture or a piece of music—what's exciting is that you're hearing the latest sentence in a conversation you've been having all your life. When you look at a painting, you don't just see that painting, you see every other picture you've ever seen. That painting is in the context of every painting you've ever seen.

This resonated with me immediately, because if we are to consider ourselves creative, and therefore a sort of artist in our fundraising roles, then we have to cast our current and future donors as the patrons of our art. And if that is true, then that means every message or appeal we send does not stand alone. That message—like the paintings that Eno describes—is only the latest sentence in a conversation the donors have been having all their lives with the charities and causes they support. This means that we fundraisers have a shared responsibility to ensure these conversations are meaningful and honest. Because if they aren't, then one bad apple could spoil the whole bunch.

As I write this, a Canadian charity called WE Charity is embroiled in controversy related to a grant from the federal government. Regardless of how that ends, the public nature of the investigation means that for hundreds of thousands, if not millions of Canadians, this story is the latest sentence in the conversation with charities they've been having all their lives, and it can't be erased.

If you've made it this far—thank you. You've opened the black box, and are a better fundraiser because of it. Your journey isn't done, and may never be, because there will always be a new mystery to unravel. Every subject and chapter of this book is just a doorway. It's up to you to build and furnish the rooms to suit your needs.

With this strong foundation of understanding, there is freedom. Freedom to never be beholden to an inherited system, because as you now know, everything is adaptable. Everything is up for debate, and there is no challenge or roadblock that you can't diagnose, dissect, or destroy.

ABOUT THE AUTHOR

Brock Warner, CFRE has over a decade of experience spanning every major nonprofit sector in Canada. As a direct marketer, he managed digital and print campaigns in healthcare, education, amateur athletics, humanitarian and domestic aid, and the environment. As a senior leader on the front lines, Brock's efforts have largely been in international development and mental health. Brock completed his undergraduate degree at Wilfrid Laurier University, and a postgraduate certification in Fundraising and Volunteer Management at Humber College in Toronto. He is a Certified Fund Raising Executive (CFRE), as well as a longstanding member of the Association of Fundraising Professionals (AFP) Greater Toronto Chapter. He has also obtained the bCRE-PRO designation for a professional-level proficiency in Blackbaud Raiser's Edge. More recently, Brock has been completing his Certificate of Leadership Practice from the Banff Centre for Arts and Creativity. Their courses emphasize new ways of thinking and doing to build purpose-driven initiatives and institutions, and are informed by artistic and Indigenous perspectives throughout the programming.